A Fresh Look at Loneliness

A Fresh Look at Loneliness

HOW TO MOVE FROM LONELINESS TO CARING

Velma Darbo Stevens

BROADMAN PRESS
Nashville, Tennessee

1981
GOLDEN GATE SEMINARY LIBRARY
Gateway Seminary Library

© Copyright 1981 • Broadman Press
All rights reserved.
4252-97
ISBN: 0-8054-5297-4
Dewey Decimal Classification: 152.4
Subject heading: LONELINESS
Library of Congress Catalog Card Number: 81-65802
Printed in the United States of America

To my dear husband

Vance

who gave me a new name

and took away my lonely times

Contents

1

Who Are the Lonely People?

Who are the lonely people? They are not hard to find. They are all around us. In fact, one of them sometimes is living inside your skin. Everyone is lonely at times. Some people are lonely most of the time.

You can find lonely people by standing on any street corner in urban America. Scan the faces of the other persons on the curb. Notice the vacant stares, the empty eyes, the expressionless mouths. These are people who look as if they were only half alive. Some of them may be absorbed in their thoughts. But the large majority are just standing there—alone in a crowd and possibly lonely.

Lonely people are not just a "special breed," persons who have not learned to make contact with others. There are such people. But they are by no means the only lonely people or even the majority of lonely people. Loneliness has become epidemic in America. One author says that it is "an almost permanent condition for millions of Americans."[1]

Lonely people include the executive on the way up who no longer talks to his wife; the young man or woman alone for the first time in an apartment complex in a large city; the suburban housewife surrounded by small children and by neighbors whom she does not know. There are lonely people among the "swingers" who spend their evenings in darkened bars, hoping for someone to talk with. Couples who have just moved for the third time in two years may be lonely. They despair of making friends before they have to take up roots again because of a job transfer. The airlines personnel who meet many people on air-planes, know very few. The salesman who has to travel all week and his wife who stays home alone may both be lonely. Don't forget the "migratory workers," a group which includes more people than just those who follow the crops. Professional sportsmen, entertainers, long-distance truck drivers, oil special-ists, and scientific engineers, as well as military personnel, are all "migratory workers." They have to travel long distances from home in order to do their work.

As we look at loneliness, it may seem that not much can be done about it, except to change one's surroundings or one's way of making a living. But this is not true. Most of the roots of loneliness are within each person. The circumstances of life can only cause long-term loneliness if the person allows them to. Just as there is a basic desire for meaningful human contact, there is a basic ability to make meaningful contacts with others.

Most lonely people spend much time thinking, *I wish I had someone to care about me.* This attitude can be changed to say, *I want to care about someone.* This simple but profound change in the depths of a person's soul can turn his or her life around! People can move from loneliness to caring. There will still be lonely periods, but loneliness will not be a fearful element in life anymore.

If it were as easy to make this change as it is to write about it, books like this one would not be needed. But many steps must be taken to make such a change in attitude.

The most important step is to recognize one's own worth—one's birthright to be a friend and to have friends. For many people, even Christians, this requires a better understanding of who human being are and how God regards them. Out of this understanding comes the power to make changes in one's life and attitudes.

This book is a practical one. Its premise is that people can change their lives if they will work at the task. So there are suggestions for changing one's ideas about oneself and others. Ideas are presented for making and keeping friends. There are steps to follow in finding and becoming a part of caring groups of persons.

The church is one of the most important of these caring groups. Sometimes the church needs to do a better job of fostering the caring groups within its structure. This book contains suggestions as to how the church may do so.

Also, there are ideas for handling one's times of loneliness in creative ways. Even for the most outgoing person, loneliness is sometimes a fact of life. In taking care of the lonely times, persons can discover new resources within themselves. Most important, they can grow into a deeper relationship with God through Christ when they are alone with him.

Finally, a chapter is devoted to becoming a caring person. The steps of change are not completed until the lonely person becomes a caring person, reaching out to other lonely human beings. Only then can persons be delivered from the fear of loneliness. Only then will the loneliness that is so much a part of our society begin to diminish.

This book will be almost useless if it is not put to use by its readers. It is much easier to think about changing surroundings and other people than to work on changing oneself. Someone has said, "We are always trying to do the impossible—to change other persons. We will not work on what is possible—changing ourselves."

In the end, what a lonely person does about loneliness is up to him or her. Practical suggestions for change make no difference until they are put into action. Such changes call for a dedication of will, of energy, and of time. But they are worth whatever it takes. No one but the lonely person can cure his or her own loneliness! But that person has within himself or herself, with the help of God, all the resources that are needed to make such changes.

Note

1. Suzanne Gordon, *Lonely in America* (New York: Simon and Schuster, 1976), p. 15.

2

What Makes People Lonely?

Janet sits at the kitchen table over her fourth cup of coffee, staring blankly into space. Her three-year-old son, Kent, sprawls in front of the television set. Her other two children are at school. Janet knows she needs to go to the supermarket for groceries, but she doesn't want to move. She feels deserted and in a hostile environment. Only the four walls of her house and the familiar furniture make her feel safe. She dreads facing all the strangers in the shopping center.

Janet and Martin recently moved to this large city in a different part of the country from where they grew up. It was a big promotion for Martin, and both were pleased to move. But Janet had not reckoned with the loneliness she would feel in a sprawling suburb filled with anonymous houses and strange faces. She cries a lot when she is alone. But she doesn't dare let Martin know how she feels. She believes he is absolutely overjoyed with his job. How could she tell him that she longs to go back where they used to live?

But Martin is not as happy as Janet supposes. A basically shy man, he has striven through the years to project the image of the hard-nosed businessman. It was partly this image that led to his promotion. In his new job, he has been given the responsibility to improve performance—to take out the "fat"—in one of the departments of the business. He feels that nobody likes him. He is afraid to make friends for fear that he will be seen as weak and unable to cope.

Janet is the only person whom Martin can trust with his

feelings. He depends very greatly on her encouragement, understanding, and sympathy. Right now he does not think he is getting much of any of these. He knows that Janet is unhappy, but
he does not know why. His parents never discussed their feelings
with each other or with their children. Martin has never learned
to open up about his feelings. He felt that his mother always
"instinctively" understood him. He expects Janet to do the
same.

Now Janet seems very withdrawn from him. He feels angry
and hurt. He knows that much of the change has come since the
move, but he does not see the connection. She has a much nicer
house than the one they left. The children are in a good school.
He does not inquire about how she spends her days. When he
comes home, he needs to tell her about his troubles.

The situation with Janet and Martin is not unusual. Many
persons, both single and married, experience many of these feelings. All people know what it means to be lonely at various times
in their lives. Some loneliness comes from social or environ-
mental changes, such as a move or a change in marital status.
Other loneliness is a product of childhood conditioning which
prevents a person from making friends. And from time to time
everyone experiences periods of aloneness or loneliness. Whatever the cause, everyone knows what it means to be lonely—and
what it feels like.

Loneliness describes the feelings persons have in the
absence of meaningful human contact. We want someone to
share our lives with, even for a few moments. Those experiences
may be as light as just having someone to laugh with over a joke
or to share the high, and low, moments of a football game. On
deeper levels, we want someone to tell our thoughts to, someone
to cry when we cry, someone who we feel really knows us. The
lack of such meaningful contacts with other persons gives rise to
feelings of loneliness.

These feelings are primarily emptiness and desolation: the way one would feel on a desert island or in solitary confinement. If loneliness is prolonged, feelings of fear, anger, distrust, envy, and self-pity will develop. These emotions are mentally and physically destructive. Persons with long-standing loneliness are more apt to overeat, overdrink, engage in drug abuse, and get such psychosomatic illnesses as ulcers and headaches.

Why does lack of personal contact have such devastating consequences? A study of babies in a hospital, conducted by Dr. René Spitz in 1945, can tell us a lot.[1] Spitz observed that the death rate among these babies was much higher than among babies kept at home. The hospitalized infants, in spite of getting adequate diets, suffered from apathy and loss of weight. He suspected that the difference lay in the personal attention which babies got from their mothers at home. In the hospital, the infants were handled only when they were fed and changed. Otherwise, they were left alone.

Spitz ordered a specific treatment of holding, cuddling, and rocking the babies for a certain length of time at intervals throughout the day. Within a short period of time, these babies became more alert, ate better, and gained both weight and strength. The death rate dropped dramatically. Spitz's conclusion was that such personal attention (meaningful human contact) was essential for both the physical and emotional well-being of the young child.

God created human beings to have fellowship with one another. The institutions of marriage, family, and community are all provided to make meaningful contact possible and actual. In some primitive societies, exclusion from the community can cause the death of the exile. He will simply sicken and die—in much the same way the babies did in the hospital. This illustrates the primary importance of community groups for human beings. Even in our advanced civilization, loneliness has been known to impel persons to suicide. Though they have not been driven out of society, they feel exiled from it. Life no longer seems worth living.

With all the institutions and groups dedicated to bringing people together, it would seem that persons need not be lonely. In America more and more people are marrying. More of us live in cities than in isolated villages or on farms. Yet loneliness seems to be more prevalent than ever.

The sad fact is that the very groups which can provide meaningful human contact—the family, marriage, and community—can also be the seedbeds of attitudes and actions that cut persons off from each other.

Flawed patterns of relating to each other are seen constantly in our families and societies. Both personal inability to relate to others and social patterns that cut persons off from one another have their roots in unhealthy attitudes in home and community.

Therefore, there is no one cause for loneliness. There is not a "loneliness virus" that can be isolated and treated. Rather, there are almost as many causes as there are persons afflicted with loneliness. But some of the roots can be identified, both in the person and in society.

Loneliness as a Personal Problem

Many persons are not equipped by background and training to make friends. The home is the model for all our later relationships. If parents are not good at making friends, very likely children will not be good at it either.

I remember in my childhood that my parents had few friends. We seemed isolated from most of our community. One day my father complained that a man he knew had not spoken to him when they passed on the street. As a teenager, I was beginning to see some of the reasons why my parents did not have friends. So I asked my father, "Well, did you speak to him?"

My father's answer was unconsciously very revealing of his

attitude: "Of course not! I don't speak to people who don't speak to me first!" He did not realize that he was forcing the initiative for simple friendship always onto the other person. He wanted his neighbor to do for him what he was unwilling to do for his neighbor.

Unfriendly attitudes that are handed on to children are suspicion of persons who are not well known, an unwillingness to share with others, and a general coldness in dealing with persons outside the family. For many years, families lived in communities where everyone was known and most people were related by blood or marriage. One could be close in such a community. With the scattering of families, such blood closeness has dissipated. And many people have not learned the skills of getting close to people to whom they feel no ties of blood or longtime acquaintance.

Many homes, also, exhibit lack of fellowship among the members. Parents may spend much time quarreling. The children never hear real conversations between their parents. The parents talk only when they are fighting. This has become their major way of communicating, of keeping in touch with each other. They are afraid to get close, to be loving and physically in contact. So they keep in touch through aggressive and combative behavior. Children in such a family may fear closeness with another human being. They unconsciously believe that closeness inevitably brings conflict, as it did in their own family.

In some homes, competition among the children is fostered rather than discouraged. Parents pit children against one another. One child's accomplishments or good behavior is held up to another with the demand that it be matched by the other child. Children who grow up in such a competitive atmosphere may adopt various attitudes toward persons later on. They may be so cowed by the competition that they will not try to establish relationships with anyone. Or they may become so competitive that the only way they know how to relate is through competition. I know a man who grew up with the idea that he had to be top dog among the boys his age. Even in his forties, he found it difficult to relate to men his age except on the tennis court or in other competitive areas.

Perhaps more devastating than these ways of relating in the home are the parents' implied—and often unconscious—attitudes toward their children. Parents in America feel a lot of pressure for their children to achieve, to succeed, to move up the ladder. From the time children begin to walk and talk, parents are anxious that the children not be backward. If they do not walk, talk, teethe, and become toilet trained at the same time as other children of the same age group, parents become quite anxious. These parents pressure children throughout their lives to do better, to do it right, to do it faster. Such children grow up with a serious lack of self-confidence and self-esteem.

Being a friend means sharing oneself with another person. People who are filled with self-doubt and self-belittling give the impression that they have nothing to share. It is not surprising that persons avoid those who exhibit such attitudes toward themselves. Everyone wants to gain something from a relationship. If someone implicitly says—by actions and attitudes—that he or she has nothing to share, others will avoid that person.

On the other hand, parents may give their children unrealistic ideas of their own importance. A man who was an only child was totally indulged by his mother. She had become disillusioned with her marriage, and she devoted all her attention to her little boy. He grew up believing that the world, especially the world of women, revolved around him. He found it hard to relate to any woman who did not give him the unreasoning devotion bestowed on him by his mother. Such persons cut off relationships with others before they actually start.

Unhealthy attitudes and poor modeling at home are carried over into marriage. The one real model for marriage and home which we have is the one each of us came from. It is not surprising that both good and bad patterns of family life are repeated generation after generation.

Also contributing to the problems of marriage is the myth that there is one person who can satisfy all my needs—physical, emotional, and social. By marrying this person, I can guarantee my own happiness. I can "live happily ever after." Such an expectation puts a heavy burden on the spouse. No one person can be all in all to another. In former generations, with extended families living in the same community, needs were passed around among grandparents, aunts, uncles, and cousins. This community of relatives helped to meet each other's needs for closeness, emotional support, advice, and companionship. Now all these needs are lumped together in the one-to-one relationship of marriage. No wonder so many marriages tear apart under the pressure!

The problem is compounded when two lonely people marry. Each one unconsciously makes this contract (never actually stated but firmly believed): "I will marry you if you will keep me from being lonely." But each one brings to the marriage more needs than resources. Each leans totally on the other for support. The reaction of the partner is helplessness, resentment, or panic. Neither one really expected to have to meet the other's needs.

Such marriages tend either to be broken openly by divorce or to become internally broken. If the partners stay together, the relationship is fragmented, cold, and distant. In either case, the children suffer the loss of close contact. Often they grow up to repeat these destructive patterns, if they marry at all.

Loneliness as a Disease of Society

Social conditions in America do not work for good relationships. In fact, looking at these conditions, one might think that they had been diabolically constructed to make people lonely.

One of the most important facts of American society is its

mobility. But enduring friendships require stability. One does not make a good friend overnight. It may take years to set up a network of loving, caring friends. Yet, very few people have the luxury of longtime residence in one place.

The average American moves fourteen times in his life. About forty million persons change addresses at least once a year. With such a fluid population, it is no wonder that few people have the chance to establish networks of friendship.

Mobility may have two different effects: Either persons tend to avoid friendships entirely or they come to specialize in instant friendships. I remember a woman, whose job called for her to travel constantly, who took the latter course. She never stayed long in any city, so she quickly got on warm terms with the persons she met. She socialized with these people, confided in them—to a certain extent—and showered them with promises of keeping in touch after she left. Of course those promises were never kept. Her sharing, too, was very superficial. People realized later that she had not revealed anything really important about herself.

This is natural, of course. Persons do not open their depths to comparative strangers. But to avoid loneliness in strange places, they set up an illusion of friendship. Since it is not based on real sharing or a growth of relationships, such a friendship withers and dies quickly after the contact is withdrawn. Persons who have to move a lot find that this kind of relating gives them some friendship but a minimum of pain when they leave. "Easy come, easy go" is the motto.

Persons who work for large corporations especially feel the need to guard against entanglement with friends in one community. Some large corporations tend to move their personnel, particularly junior executives, from one place to another with painful frequency. A 1969 study found that two-thirds of corporate managers aged 25-40 had moved at least one time every three years.[2] One in five had moved at least once every year So the commonsense attitude among these families is not to put down roots. What would be the use if they know they will move again in a year or two? Such families may spend most of their lives being lonely.

Another result of mobility is that modern families are cut off from their extended families and from the communities in which they grew up. Very few people marry the "girl (or boy) next door" any more. Instead, Helen from Montana meets Joe from Indiana at a college in Missouri. They marry and move to Texas where Joe gets a job. They are now isolated from their families and friends back home and also from the friends they made mutually in college.

Not only do they leave family and friends behind but also they tend to grow apart from their own ties. A woman in her thirties said to me regretfully, "I don't feel as if I belong to my family anymore. They all seem to look at things differently from the way Jim and I do." The result of this woman's living in a different area and having very different experiences was a sense of isolation from her family. Other factors that cause estrangement are getting more education than the parents, moving to an urban area from a rural one, and working in an impersonal corporation where much mobility is the rule. Therefore, in our mobile society, often the only enduring family relationship is husband-wife. This is another reason for the great pressure exerted between spouses to be all things to each other.

In contrast to the way mobility contributes to loneliness, consider the Mexican-American migratory farm workers in South Texas. Whole villages along the Rio Grande empty in the springtime so that the people can follow the crops. These people, for about six months of the year, live a seemingly rootless existence. Yet they have amazingly strong roots.

For one thing, they travel with families and neighbors. So they do not feel isolated, even though they are in strange areas, far away from home.

Also, they have strong ties to their own communities. About 48 percent own their homes. This rate of ownership is higher than for the general United States population.[3] Their houses are generally simple, square bungalows of probably four rooms. But they are colorfully painted, and most yards contain vegetable and flower gardens, along with chickens and pets. When the workers have finished their migratory season, they head for home to South Texas to take up community life again.

Another social condition that increases loneliness is the large-scale move to suburban living. The suburbs were supposed to combine the convenience of city living with the pleasures of country living. But one element was left out—community. In most suburbs, places for communal gathering, such as parks, neighborhood centers, or churches, are not within walking distance. So suburban dwellers have become also commuters within the community—driving to stores, churches, and schools.

Because the communities are large—often as large as small cities—one seldom meets friends and neighbors even at shopping centers or supermarkets. In fact, it is a pleasant surprise to run into a friend in such a place.

In the suburbs, even close neighbors can be strangers. It is commonplace for persons not even to know the names of families within three houses of them. "Privacy fences" cut people off from next-door neighbors.

In some cities, officials conduct campaigns to encourage neighbors to watch out for one another in order to discourage suburban crime. Frequently daring criminals have moved a van up to a house and emptied it without disturbance from neighbors. These persons may have noticed the van. But they knew so little about their neighbors that they simply assumed the people were moving out.

When we realize that 37.6 percent of all Americans live in suburbs, it is easy to understand how much such conditions contribute to loneliness.[4]

We are also seeing a sharp increase in apartment living. High-rise apartments and apartment complexes are being built rapidly. Here the isolation is even more complete. Persons who have to live very close to one another try to keep emotional distance, since they cannot keep physical distance. There seems to be no other way to preserve privacy.

Apartment living is also impersonal living. All apartments look alike basically, even though builders strive for unique looks for different complexes. There is a sense of transience about an apartment. In fact, some younger apartment dwellers rent furniture rather than buying it. Then, if they have to move to another apartment or another city, they simply turn their furniture back in!

Many of the persons who live in apartments are singles, either never married, widowed, or divorced. Single living is becoming an acceptable option in our society. But it still has a very low status with some people. In a couple-oriented society, it seems unbelievable that anyone would choose to live alone. Many never-married persons feel that they are "oddballs" to their married acquaintances. And formerly married persons are generally objects of pity because they have lost their partners. So single living contributes to loneliness.

Beneath all these trends in social living lie certain attitudes of society that foster loneliness.

One is the fact that ours is a very competitive society. It begins in school, continues when persons look for jobs or mates, and is seen most clearly in business. Supply and demand is the creed by which most Americans operate. "There may not be enough for both you and me, so it's important for me to get mine first. If there is enough left, I'll be glad for you to get yours, too." Such a basic attitude fosters selfishness, greed, and a fear that we will run out of basic resources.

We are becoming increasingly a pluralistic society. Jehovah's Witnesses, agnostics, and Zen Buddhists exist in the same neighborhood with Baptists, Catholics, and Presbyterians. There is no longer a shared understanding about moral standards for children and youth. Next-door neighbors may have values that are as far apart as total license to do anything is from the strictest discipline. Persons have widely differing views on many issues, such as abortion, authority in the family, women's rights, and governmental control. It is easy to get a feeling of isolation when neighbors don't look at life the same way.

A third trend is a strong emphasis on individual freedom. This trend has arisen in the last ten to fifteen years, since the late sixties. Great value is placed on independence from others and on individual rights.

A young man, protesting the registration for military service in 1980, was asked his reasons. He answered harshly, "I don't want the government getting its dirty fingers on me—or anybody else getting control of me." His total concern seemed to be for himself and his freedom of movement.

Although this extreme stress on freedom is new, individualism—refusal to be dependent on others—has always been a strong component of American life. Americans are oriented toward privacy and independence. Many of our technological advances are attempts to make persons self-sufficient. A housewife need not step outside the door in order to wash and dry clothes or to find out what is going on in the world. The person who drives to work does so alone, by choice. Surveys of workers find that, even with high gasoline cost and periodic shortages, persons emphatically prefer to go to work alone. One observation, heard frequently, is that this is the only time during the day when the worker can be alone.

But all these trends toward independence and freedom cut the person off from one important need—the need to relate to others. It is possible to be very lonely while driving around in a fine car, sitting before a television set with one's spouse in a well-furnished family room, or proclaiming one's freedom to do your own thing.

The price of this freedom is loneliness. Even more, the person who admits that he or she does need other people is judged to be weak. So loneliness is compounded with shame over being lonely when everyone else seems to be having such a good time being free.

Loneliness as a Part of Being Human

No matter how outgoing we are, how able to make friends, we cannot avoid periods of loneliness. Some loneliness will be temporary, related to being in a strange place or surrounded by strangers. There may be loneliness related to one's situation in life: being a migratory worker or having just experienced the breaking of a marriage relationship through divorce or death.

There is also a basic loneliness which comes from our being human. We long to be completely known by another person, but that is impossible. We do not even know ourselves completely. There is, then, a kind of aching void which is never totally filled.

This kind of loneliness can be creative. It drives us to make contact with others. It urges us to continue to try to understand ourselves. It compels us to seek God, for he alone can understand the depths which we can never understand in ourselves.

While looking at the causes of loneliness, it is important to understand what loneliness is not. Many people mistake other symptoms for loneliness, and they try in vain to treat these as one would treat loneliness.

Loneliness is not being alone. A group of us stood at the entrance to Muir Woods, the magnificent redwood forest outside San Francisco. We had just come from a conference where the importance of human relationships was being stressed. One of the men in the group said, "How could Muir have lived so long alone? How could he have stood the loneliness?"

None of us had an answer then. But as we penetrated deeper into the forest, we begin to understand. We sensed the grandeur of the centuries-old trees. We listened to the quiet murmur of a brook slipping among the rocks and through the ferns. We watched the brilliant blue western jay as he busied himself among the branches. Obviously, what Muir had found in the woods was not loneliness, but solitude.

Solitude expresses the ability of the person to find communion with himself, with nature, and with God without the presence of other persons. A poet, living alone in the Maine woods, is quoted as saying, "The worst part of what I experience is loneliness. The best part of what I experience is solitude."

Loneliness is not being a "loner." Some persons are more comfortable being alone. They do not feel the need of others. In fact, they do not want to be with others. So they, being alone, are really not lonely.

Loneliness is not nostalgia. Memories of the past, especially of happy times, may bring wishes for those times again. The person may exaggerate the happiness of those remembered moments and imagine that he was never lonely at such times. These memories are usually connected with special times of the year—anniversaries, birthdays, or holidays. If one is realistic, however, he will acknowledge that such times were not always as glorious as memory paints them.

The causes of loneliness are many and varied. They extend from personal conditioning to social conditions. Nearly any person afflicted with loneliness will be able to discover several causes for the feeling. In fact, each person might have a unique combination of causes.

If you are a lonely person, it is important for you to isolate the causes of your loneliness. Read back over this chapter. Find the personal and social elements of loneliness which you know are present in your life. Write these down; it is easy to forget them if you do not. Later in this book you will find ways of coping with the various causes of loneliness.

You can change some of these causes. Others you cannot change, but you can change your reaction to them. Self-knowledge is the first step. Too many people try to cope with loneliness by dealing with the wrong things. They imagine, for example, that changing their environment will automatically reduce their loneliness. But we all carry our own environment along when moving. One's way of looking at the world and relating to people does not change simply through moving to another community.

But the good news is that you can change yourself! It is a myth that adults do not change. So long as you are living, you are capable of growing, and growing means change. Often this growth is so quiet and gradual that it is hard to see changes until they come to bloom in the personality.

I saw this dramatically illustrated in my backyard one spring. I had several fruit trees, some old, some young. Summer had been hot and dry and winter extremely bitter cold. Some of the old trees and some of the young trees had not survived. So, at the tag end of winter, I told my friend Tom, who does my yard work, that I would want several trees taken out. I pointed them out to him: an ancient plum, a diseased pear, a young peach, and an old peach.

About two months later, Tom came to take out the trees. I had not looked closely at them in the interim. I went around with him, pointing out again the trees that were to be cut: the ancient plum, the diseased pear, the young peach, the old peach . . . but no! The old peach, which had shown every outward sign of being dead, was putting out leaf buds! Without my seeing what was happening, it had begun to grow again. Its growth became visible when the changes were seen.

For the Christian lonely person, God has promised his help in many ways. God always works on the side of healthy, growing relationships between people. He has provided all kinds of resources for those who are willing to work to change themselves.

Notes

1. René Spitz, "Hospitalism, Genesis of Psychiatric Conditions in Early Childhood," *Psychoanalytic Study of the Child,* 1:53-74, 1945.
2. Vance Packard, *A Nation of Strangers* (New York: David McKay Company, 1972), p. 19.
3. Ibid., p. 65.
4. Gordon, *Lonely in America,* p. 101.

3

God's Word to Lonely People

When I was a child, my father had a strange young friend. He had lived in Palestine for a number of years and was converted there. He felt a call to preach. So the missionary who had led him to Christ persuaded him to come to our city to attend seminary. My father became acquainted with him because both men were Norwegian.

The thing I remember most about this young man was that he was always singing, in his broken English, "No longer lonely! No longer lonely! For Jesus is the friend of friends to me." Yet he was the loneliest person I knew. He did not do well in seminary and made few friends. About midsemester, he dropped out of school and left the city.

Looking back, I think that he was a very lonely man. He found solace in the fact that Jesus was his friend. But he did not learn from Jesus how to make earthly friends, even among Christians.

This man stands in my mind as an illustration of many lonely Christians. They have accepted God's blessings as they relate to heaven, but not on earth.

There is the woman who, when told that she is "unique in all the world," laughs nervously and says, "It's a good thing! I'm such a poor specimen that I wouldn't want anyone else to be like me."

There is the man who, when told that God loves him absolutely and unconditionally, thinks to himself, *But I'm sure God would love me more if I were a tither.*

There are many people like my father's friend who can accept the love and friendship of Jesus but do not know how to find friends among Jesus' followers. These persons do not see the vast resources God has provided for them to have fellowship with other human beings. But it is God's purpose that his children should live in harmony and fellowship with many other persons. The New Testament is filled with examples of such friendship. It gives numerous suggestions for making and preserving friends.

One problem that lonely people have in relating to others is their low self-esteem, like the woman quoted earlier. They find it hard to believe that anyone would want to relate to them as a friend. They do not recognize their own potential to make friends. They feel that they must become somebody different in order for people to like them. God has a special word for these people.

God's First Word: Personal Worth

Every person is of infinite worth. That truth is emphasized over and over in the Bible, beginning with the first chapter of Genesis.

God said, "Let us make man in our image" (Gen. 1:27). To be in the image of God means a lot of things—reason, will, spirit, ability to relate to God. But basically it means that each person is unique. If a person is in God's image, then there can be no duplicates. God does not make two snowflakes or two maple leaves exactly alike. We should not suppose, then, that he would make two human beings alike. Each person is special, unique in all the world.

This truth is borne out by biological facts. Geneticists tell us that the chances of two people being born with exactly the same set of genes are astronomically small. Even projecting back through history and forward into the future, it would be well-nigh impossible for there ever to be two persons born exactly alike.

Even identical twins, born of the same genes, are not the same. Their fingerprints and even their voice patterns are distinctive.

Being uniquely created in the image of God is good news for lonely people. By living out of that special blend of qualities, the lonely person has much to offer to a relationship. By being authentically oneself, he or she can confidently relate to other people.

Being made in the image of God is not the only truth about personal worth. An even greater truth is that God loves each person whom he has made. This is great news for lonely people! Each of us longs for someone to love us unconditionally. We want to know that we are loved even when we don't deserve it or feel that we don't deserve it.

There are two great words about God's unconditional love in the New Testament: Romans 5:8: "But God shows his love for us in that while we were yet sinners Christ died for us."[1] (Read Rom. 5:6-10 to get the full impact.) Ephesians 2:4-5: "God, . . . out of the great love with which he loved us, even when we were dead through our trespasses" (RSV). In both these verses, the emphasis is on our unworthiness to be loved. Who is willing to die for a bad person, a sinner? Yet Christ died for us. Who can truly love a dead body? Yet God loved us when we were as dead spiritually as any corpse rotting in the grave.

This is not a talking-about love. It is love in action. It was love that caused God to give his dearest companion, his Son, in order to have relationship with sinful human beings. A God who loves enough to do that obviously thinks that the human beings for whom he sacrificed his Son are worth a tremendous lot. Anyone who puts himself down, either to himself or to others, is not just downgrading himself. He is also downgrading God. If God has declared, by word and act, that I am of infinite worth to him, then I must adopt that attitude toward myself. Otherwise I am implying that God is a liar, that I am not of infinite worth.

Nor did God stop with what he did in Christ for us human beings. He brought us into his family, so that we are called "children of God." This is a revolutionary idea. Among the religions of the world, there are doctrines of relationships with a supreme being. But Christianity alone declares that all human beings can be children of God through faith in Jesus Christ. Not even the Jews would make such a claim, except for the nation as a whole.

This is great news for lonely people. It frees them from the need to "live up to" their parents' expectations. All parents, consciously or unconsciously, load down their children with demands. They may expect their children to excel in business, make good marriages, be beautiful or athletic. They may even put negative expectations on their children. They may expect their children to turn out stupid, unsuccessful, awkward, unable to relate to others. These expectations get communicated in various subtle ways. The children feel bound internally by these expectations.

Sometimes the demands are what the children perceived their parents to want. Perhaps the parents did not intend what the child thinks was expected of him. Yet it is difficult to get away from the inner demands. The child internalizes what he thinks the parents want and tries to live up to it.

Being a child of God delivers a person from false or unreasonable expectations. God does not set up demands based on what other people want or expect. What he wants from every child of his is that each person should live up to the uniqueness of his or her own personality. These are endowments given from God. Naturally, he wants them to be lived to the full. This desire of God is expressed as being "conformed to the image of his Son" (Rom. 8:29, RSV).

Many Christians get the idea that this means that their individuality must be smothered and their personalities destroyed. They do not see how being totally themselves and being conformed to the image of Jesus can be compatible. But they are!

God does not want little "clones" of Jesus. In fact, it would be presumptuous for any of us to think that one person could be like Jesus. It is all of us together who will be like him (Eph. 4:13). To accomplish that, each person must live out his or her uniqueness.

When I think of Christians forming the image of Jesus Christ, I remember the beautiful stained-glass window in my church showing the welcoming Christ. It took hundreds of pieces of glass, of various shapes and colors, to compose this window. This is a picture of how we shall be "conformed to the image" of Jesus, I believe. Each person will contribute his or her own bit.

But suppose one person— a triangular piece of blue glass, let's say—wants to be a square piece of red. This person will strive hard to be different from the original design but will not succeed. Even if this person became a square piece of red glass, there might well be no place for it in the design. Meanwhile, there would be a void where a triangular piece of blue was intended to go—and the picture of Christ would be incomplete.

So persons need to assert their true worth and to seek to grow in their uniqueness. It is out of such growing that truly creative, long-lasting relationships come.

This, however, leads to another problem for lonely people. Many of them do not have a clear idea of what it takes to have a creative relationship. They may have lived in families where there was suspicion, anger, coldness, or lack of love. If they are married, they probably carried this pattern into their own families. Whatever friendships they have are tainted by this unhealthy modeling. God has a special word for these people.

God's Second Word: Personal Relationships

God himself sets the model for relationships between persons. There is no true relationship without love. God is love: This is one of the best ways to describe the nature of God. We not only experience his love but also we learn from him how to love one another. "In this the love of God was made manifest among us, that God sent his only Son into the world, so that we might live through him. . . . Beloved, if God so loved us, we also ought to love one another" (1 John 4:9,11, RSV).

This progression of the love relationship is clearly set out for us in the two great commandments: "You shall love the Lord your God with all your heart, and with all your soul, and with all your mind. . . . You shall love your neighbor as yourself" (Matt. 22:37,39, RSV). First God loves us. Then we love God—with all our being. Then we learn from God how to love on a human level. First we learn to love ourselves aright. Then we learn to love other persons as healthily as we love ourselves.

Dr. James Landes, writing about the way we love ourselves healthily, has some helpful insights:

Love has been well defined as devotion to the ends of God in a human personality. Self-love then is devotion to the ends of God in my own personality. If love for myself is of that quality, I will work to become what God means me to be. I will have a sense of direction in my life. I will impose discipline upon myself. I will, with God's help, develop the powers that God has entrusted to me. I must care enough for myself to develop my powers to the limit of my opportunity.

. . . Unless I am devoted to the ends of God in my own personality, I cannot be devoted to the ends of God in my neighbor's personality. If I love myself aright, I shall desire for my neighbor what I desire for myself—not necessarily the same things, for they might be useless to him, but I shall desire for him whatever will help him to find his own self-fulfillment.[2]

Jesus, of course, was the absolute model for creative relationships. He enjoyed constant fellowship with his Father. He was devoted to "the ends of God" in his own personality. He built warm and enduring friendships with his own followers. He spoke of these relationships as being "in" one another. In his prayer for his disciples, recorded in John 17, Jesus asked "that they may be one even as we are one, I in them and thou in me, that they may become perfectly one" (vv. 22-23, RSV). Think of the times persons have longed for such oneness: with husband or wife, with children or parents, with relatives and friends. Perfect oneness is not possible except with God through Jesus Christ. And oneness on a human level is possible only by relating as Jesus Christ taught and as God empowers.

Here is a third problem for lonely people. Most of them do not feel that they have the power, the ability, to make friends. They are lonely, often desperately so. But they lack the strength, the courage, to move out into the wilderness of human relationships. They see no way to break the vicious circle in which they are trapped. God has a special word for these people.

God's Third Word: Personal Resources

It is characteristic of God that when he helps persons he does so in a personal way. When he delivered the children of Israel from Egypt, he worked through Moses. When he chose to redeem all mankind, he did so, not by some impersonal means, but through his Son. And when he offers day-by-day help in living, he does so through the person of his Spirit.

To have God's Holy Spirit living constantly within us is the greatest resource we can have. Bank accounts can be exhausted, mental resources can dry up, advisers and counselors can fail. But to have the total resources of God available twenty-four hours a day is to have on tap all of God's "riches in glory." The Bible makes specific promises as to what the Spirit can do for us.

He will be our constant Companion. There is no need for devastating loneliness when we are conscious of the Spirit's presence with us. This is the reason why my father's friend could sing, "No longer lonely." There will be lonely times. But the comforting presence of the Spirit can overcome earthly loneliness.

When Jesus promised to send the Spirit, he said, "When I go, you will not be left all alone; I will come back to you" (John 14:18).[3] The word translated "comfortless" in the KJV and "all alone" in the TEV is literally "orphaned." No one needs to feel all alone in the world. There will always be one other with him: the Spirit of God.

As a constant companion, the Spirit is always available to supply guidance and wisdom for daily living. He does not force this guidance on us. We can have the indwelling Spirit and still go on our bumbling way. But we don't have to! Over and over in the New Testament, Christians are urged to let the Spirit of God lead them in daily living, not to "quench the Spirit," not to "grieve" the Spirit. The Spirit will do with us what we allow him to do. But even when we don't listen to him, he is still present, still available, and undiscourageable.

The Spirit of God gives inner courage, strength, and confidence. Lonely people often feel unable to move out of their situation, even when they know the steps to take. The Spirit provides the needed "motive power." Paul described the Spirit's work this way. "The Spirit that God has given us does not make us timid; instead, his Spirit fills us with power, love, and self-control" (2 Tim. 1:7, TEV). Such confidence can free persons from the bonds of inhibition and fear that have come from their childhood or their past experiences. "Where the Spirit of the Lord is present, there is freedom" (2 Cor. 3:17, TEV).

One reason for this confidence and sense of freedom is that the Spirit continually reassures us that we are truly the children of God. We are apt to believe this truth more with our heads than with our hearts. Loving in the consciousness of our child-Father relationship with God makes us free and confident. "Because you are sons, God has sent the Spirit of his Son into our hearts, crying, 'Abba! Father!' " (Gal. 4:6, RSV).

As the Spirit works in our lives, he provides us with the qualities of living that nourish good, wholesome relationships. "The Spirit produces love, joy, peace, patience, kindness, goodness, faithfulness, humility, and self-control" (Gal. 5:22-23, TEV). All these are traits that make it possible for persons to live in harmony and warmth with each other. Consider these qualities individually:

Love, joy, and peace all relate to God and Christ in the New Testament. Love is God's kind of love, which we are to express to others. Joy is the overflowing sense of happiness that is unrelated to outward circumstances. Peace also does not require outward harmony in order to be felt. It is the peace which Jesus said he was leaving to his disciples, no matter what the world did to them (see John 14:27).

Patience, kindness, and goodness relate to the way we treat each other. Patience means to be "long-tempered." It describes the person who does not have "a short fuse." It helps one bear with another's faults. Kindness and goodness both describe our treatment of other people. Kindness may be thought of as an attitude toward others, while goodness is that attitude expressed in action.

Faithfulness, humility, and self-control are qualities that make it possible for the Christian to live out the first six qualities. Faithfulness is the quality of trustworthiness. The Christian can be trusted to carry out his Lord's commands and to be honest and reliable with other persons. Humility is also rendered "gentleness." It refers to the person who, having inner strength, does not need constantly to prove himself to others. He is like the German shepherd who can lie quietly while a little poodle yaps at him over the fence. The big dog has no need to prove his power to the little fellow. Self-control also relates to inner strength. It is the power of a person's will. One's will makes it possible to keep control of wayward impulses or selfish instincts.

Since these traits are gifts, or fruits, of the Spirit, they do not need to be hacked out by tireless effort. These traits are part of the nature of the Spirit of God. Through his living in our lives, he gradually infuses us with these same qualities, as we let him. It is like two people living in close harmony for many years, who begin to talk and act and think alike. They do not lose their individuality. But their personalities are changed as they absorb each other's qualities. The Spirit does not want to change our personalities. But he wants us to live happily and harmoniously in this world, as well as in the next, and he supplies the qualities to make this possible.

One further word: We do not need to do anything to "get" the Spirit. He comes to us as our birthright. When we are born again through faith in Jesus Christ, the Spirit of God enters our lives. He will never leave. He is as much a part of our beings because we are spiritually newborn as our will and intellect are part of our beings because we are born human.

How do we avail ourselves of all the benefits which God has promised us? They do not come automatically. We must do our part, and that is stated in one word: faith.

We understand faith when it is related to our becoming Christians in the first place. But for many people, especially those who are lonely, faith sometimes has a hollow ring. They are Christians. They long to have the kinds of lives "victorious" Christians describe. But things don't seem to happen for them the way they do for these other Christians. If faith is what is needed, they do not think they have it or enough of it.

Faith for daily living is really no different from the faith that brought us to Christ in the first place. It is defined this way in Hebrews 11:1: "To have faith is to be sure of the things we hope for, to be certain of the things we cannot see" (TEV). Surely that describes what happened when we accepted Christ. We had no visible evidence that yielding our lives to him would bring salvation. There was no document dropped from the heavens to tell us that God would accept our faith in his Son. We had to take all those promises on faith. We knew people for whom these promises had proved true. Yet we could not be sure—absolutely sure—that the same thing would happen to us. But when we trusted, the miracle happened.

So it is with the promises God gives us day by day. We can be sure of what we hope will happen as we trust God. We can be certain that what we do not yet see will come to pass.

Our true assurance is not in what we see or what we do, but in God, in whom we believe. We cannot see him. We know by faith that he exists. And we know that he does not lie. Part of an early statement of faith says, "If we are not faithful, he remains faithful, because he cannot be false to himself" (2 Tim. 2:13, TEV). If he is not false to himself, he will never be false to any person. This is the bottom line: This is why we can have faith in God for every need of our lives, not just for our eternal salvation.

How does faith work in our lives? Jesus' illustration of the mustard seed can help us at this point. He said that if anyone had the faith of a grain of mustard seed, he could move a tree from one place to another (Luke 17:5-6). In other words, he could make impossible things happen.

The point is not the size of the mustard seed. Jesus probably chose it because it was one of the tiniest seeds he knew. The important thing is the power in the mustard seed. Although the smallest seed in the garden, the plant which grows from it is one of the largest—so big that even the birds can nest in its branches.

Most people, looking at a mustard seed, would think it of very small importance. Their question would be, What can so small a seed amount to? But the person of faith, looking at the same seed, would see the potential in it. He would see, not a dry, tiny seed, but a great, spreading plant. So Jesus said that faith is a matter of concentrating on the potential, not on what is presently seen. The person who puts her whole attention on what

God has promised and believes that it will come to pass is like a person who plants a mustard seed. Faith is hope in action.

Faith is necessary for changing one's habits of mind and action. The major emphasis of this book is that lonely people can change, so that they will be no longer lonely. But changing one's inner habits is a long and difficult task. It takes the "faith of a grain of mustard seed" for that to be accomplished. The lonely person can persist in the change exercises suggested in this book so long as he or she keeps a steady eye on the harvest. It takes faith—"hope in action" —to believe that such changes can bring about the harvest of friendship and fellowship that lonely people desire.

Notes

1. From the Revised Standard Version of the Bible, copyrighted 1946, 1952, © 1971, 1973. Subsequent quotations are marked RSV.
2. *Baptist Standard,* August 6, 1980, p. 7. Used by permission of the author.
3. This quotation is from the *Good News Bible,* the Bible in Today's English Version. Old Testament: Copyright © American Bible Society 1976; New Testament: Copyright © American Bible Society 1966, 1971, 1976. Used by permission. Subsequent quotations are marked TEV.

4

The Church as the
Caring Community

God has provided another resource for human beings through Jesus Christ; that is the church. It is through the church that many of the resources which were stated in the last chapter are made actual. God does not work with persons in isolation. Relationships—between himself and his people, among those who belong to him, and between Christians and all other people —are important elements in his plan for saving the world.

Just as a human baby needs a family in which to grow to maturity, Christians need a home in which to grow. The church provides that home. The worth of the individual, the love of God, the fruits of the Spirit are all realized in the fellowship of the church. Healthy relationships are nourished as the church carries out the will of the Father.

The church is the one institution that can absorb all ages and conditions of humankind. It brings all these persons together into a relationship of love and unity under the lordship of Christ and the authority of God the Father.

Before a presidential election, a pastor was asked whether he would work to get the new president (if a certain man won) into his church. His reply expresses the deepest principles of the church of Jesus Christ: "We are here . . . to be a servant to anyone whom God sends to us and we will attempt to make welcome any person, whether he is of low estate or the highest office in the country."[1]

In my own life, the church has been one of the greatest sources of fellowship and growth. I have found family there. I have found opportunities for service which widely expanded my horizons and also brought me many friends. I know many people who have been lonely and have found a refuge in the church.

However, the church is not a perfect institution. Many people have wrong ideas about it, based on their past experiences. So the responses to the church are widely diverse.

A couple visited the morning worship service of a large church. They came late and sat toward the back. As soon as the service was over, they hastily left. Later they complained to the church members who had invited them that no one had spoken to them at the service. They felt that the church was "very cold."

Another couple was looking for a church that really "preached the gospel." During the course of one Sunday morning, they slipped into—and out of—three churches in a downtown city area. They found something wrong with the service in each church, either with the hymns, the order of worship, or the preaching. They said that they did not believe there were any really "spiritual" churches in the town.

A widower called a volunteer organization to ask for some help with his loneliness. The volunteer asked him, among other things, whether he belonged to a church. "No," was his reply. "I was saved by watching an evangelist on TV. But I've never gone to a church."

Two young people who attended a small denominational college were completely turned off by the types of Christians they found there. These people, products of the late 60s radicalism, determined to have nothing to do with any church. After their marriage, they tended to make friends with other persons like themselves. But they became increasingly lonely. Still they refused to consider even trying to relate to a church. They pointed out all the shortcomings of the churches in their city.

A woman felt completely ostracized by the church in her former hometown after her divorce. In the city where she presently lived, she saw a retreat for divorced persons announced. She attended the retreat sponsored by a church and found much help and fellowship. But she did not continue to attend the church. She still felt that there would be persons in the church who would snub her.

A woman who was suddenly widowed declared that she could not have gone on without her church. She said that her Sunday School class was the greatest source of strength to her.

A family with three children moved to a new city. As soon as they got settled, they began visiting churches. They were looking for one, they said, which would meet the growing needs of their children. The parents felt that they could find fellowship in any church which would minister to their children.

A young couple was living in a university town where the man was working on a doctor's degree. He was very busy with his schoolwork, and his wife had a full-time job. They knew they would not be in the community long. But they got totally involved in their church. They were so much a part of the programs of the church that everyone expressed deep regret when the man finished his work and they moved to another city.

A very shy young woman was attending worship services, not getting involved in other parts of the church program. Someone, hearing her sing in church, recruited her for the choir. This gave a new dimension to her life. Soon she was enthusiastically involving herself in many parts of the church program.

A couple were having marital problems. They did not want to get counseling from a secular psychotherapist. So they went to a pastoral counselor. As their marriage improved, they began to look for new friends. They found these in the Sunday School department of the church. These friends also supported their efforts at building a sound marriage.

All these examples—which are true—illustrate varying attitudes toward the church. They also show the church's various attitudes toward persons. These seem to be a "mixed bag" of good and poor relationships between persons and the church and between the church and those to whom it should minister. Why are there such widely varying attitudes toward the church? What are the purposes of the church in relation to persons who need its ministries? How can the church best carry out these purpose?

First, it is necessary to understand what the church is and what it is not. There are many erroneous ideas about the church. By understanding the basic purpose of the church as Christ established it, we can weed out the wrong ideas. Then we should be able to look clearly at what the church can do for lonely persons.

In the beginning, Christ established the church to be a new kind of community. In it there were to be no distinctions by race, sex, age, nationality, social class, or economic status. Its purposes were to continue to carry on his work in the world and to provide a place of acceptance and fellowship where persons could grow spiritually.

Two descriptions of the church from the New Testament sum up these purposes. The church is called *the body of Christ* (1 Cor. 12:27) and *the household of faith* (Gal. 6:10), or *the family of God*.

As the body of Christ, the church continues to do in the world what Jesus did when he was on earth. The church preaches the gospel, does good, teaches disciples, witnesses to the saving power of God, and seeks to carry out God's will on earth. As the family of God, the church provides a home base for the children of God. It gives them nurture and discipline, a sense of belonging, fellowship with each other, and a shared sense of purpose and history.

If the church did all these things all the time and did them perfectly, there would be no problem. There would be ministries to lonely persons. There would be little room for misunderstanding the functions of the church. There would be opportunities for growth among the members. There would be a constant in-flow of new members.

But it is just not that simple. The church is, if you will, a hybrid. Conceived in heaven, it is lived out on earth. Commissioned by Christ, it is populated with human beings. Even though they are saved, they are not yet perfect. Nor is the church of which they are a part.

The church is both an organism (as related to God) and an organization (as related to the world). From God's point of view, the church is an organism. That means that it is a living body made up of separate but mutually dependent parts. In a body there are distinct parts, but they cannot exist apart from one another. This is the way the members of the church look to God.

From the world's point of view, the church is an organization. That means that it is a systematic social structure made up of independent parts. Since the parts are independent, members may move in and out of the structure without damage to it. The church is also related to the world by being a nonprofit organization. Even in a country where there is separation of church and state, the church has to answer to the state in many areas. Also, as an organization, the church pays a staff, provides services, maintains a building, devises a budget, and collects money.

The tension between spiritual body and social organization was brought strongly home to me in my own church not long ago. We had been revising our bylaws. Many of these were concerned with spiritual matters: the ministry of the leaders of the church, the ways the church accepts members, and the programs of the church. But other bylaws were concerned with secular affairs: finances, hiring and firing of employees, and the church's status as a nonprofit organization.

As we prepared for the vote, our pastor summed up the relation between the spiritual and the secular aspects of the church. He discussed the parliamentary procedures by which he would moderate the business meeting—all secular rules. Then he added, "I will not hesitate to rule out of order any person who is acting in an unchristian manner during the discussion or the voting. It is important not just that we express our thoughts, but how we express our thoughts. We are a church of Jesus Christ, not just an organization. We have an obligation to act as Christians toward each other during this meeting."

The problem, as we look at the church, is that many people see it as totally spiritual or as totally human. A person who sees it as totally spiritual may be disillusioned. It is not perfect, but perfection is expected of it. On the other hand, a person who sees the church as totally human may expect too little of it. That person may write the church off without looking deeply enough to see its spiritual dimensions.

It would be better for everyone—the members of the church and those who need its ministries—if the church were viewed the way God looks at it. God sees the church as it is and as it will become.

This was the way Jesus looked at Simon Peter just before the disciple betrayed him. Jesus warned Peter that he was in danger of yielding to temptation. Then he added: "I have prayed for you that your faith may not fail; and when you have turned again, strengthen your brethren" (Luke 22:32, RSV). Jesus clearly saw that Peter would betray him (v. 34). But he prayed that Peter's faith would remain intact, even in the midst of his weakness and denial. If that happened, Peter could "turn again." Jesus knew Peter's potential for leadership. He saw Peter in terms of what he could become, not just in terms of his present weakness.

So God sees the church. He suffers over it when there are church fights or splits or when the church practices injustice toward persons. But he never takes his Holy Spirit away from the church. Through the Spirit he is always calling the church back to its high purpose: to be the body of Christ and the family of God in the world.

If both church members and others looked at the church in this way, a number of other wrong ideas would be dispelled. Some of these are:

(1) That the church is a magic "open door" for persons to find relationships. Just sitting in the church pew on a Sunday morning does not guarantee fellowship. It takes active participation on the part of the ones who desire fellowship to achieve it even in the church.

(2) That the church must be filled with mature, "finished" Christians who do not have faults, in order for it to be effective. The church, like a family, is composed of persons of all stages of maturity, both spiritual and personal. As these persons relate to one another, the membership grows in wisdom and in love for one another.

(3) That the church's program is not adequate to meet the needs of persons outside it. Some people think that "special" groups or programs need to be set up in order to meet human need. Actually, the church as it presently exists contains enough diversity of ministries to meet the needs of persons within it and without it.

(4) That the church exists only in a building. The church's most visible expression is in a building, where a specific group of people meet at various times each week. But wherever two or more persons meet who are Christians, the church is there. Jesus said, "Where two or three are gathered together in my name, there am I in the midst of them." Persons who are part of Christ's body can meet, relate, and have fellowship in many ways and many places. One does not have to "go to church" in order to find warm fellowship and a family relationship.

Now let us consider how the church functions when it is acting like the body of Christ and the family of God.

The Church as the Body of Christ

In the New Testament, the church is pictured as making up the body of Christ, with him as the head. His mind and will motivate and direct the body. All the members of the church are therefore members of the body. Each has a distinct ability and function, and each is necessary to the life and health of the body.

This picture emphasizes four characteristics: the worth of each individual, the diversity among the members, the interdependence of the members, and the obedience of the members to the head.

Consider the worth and diversity of the members. Whenever a body loses one of its members, there is real suffering for the whole person. This suffering is as much emotional as it is physical. We cannot imagine ourselves functioning as we should without all our parts.

All the diverse parts of the body are likewise necessary. Paul's illustration of the foot and the ear which thought they were not part of the body because they were not a hand or an eye is both amusing and enlightening (1 Cor. 12:14-21). There are many different parts in the body, and all are necessary.

To understand better the importance of all the different members of the body, imagine that you were ordered to give up one part of your body. You could choose the part, but it had to be a working part. What would you select to be destroyed? One of your eyes, a lung, a kidney, an arm, your liver, the pituitary gland? Just so, every diverse member of the body of Christ is essential for the healthy working of the body.

These thoughts also emphasize the interdependence of the members. Every part of the body depends on every other part. Respiration, heartbeat, digestion, elimination, blood circulation, and the functioning of the glands must all stay in good working order. If not, every part of the body suffers.

Such interdependence is not random or undirected. The head controls all the functioning of the body. Even the automatic functioning is probably dependent on the mind at a subconscious level. So all the members of the church are dependent of their head—the Lord Christ. Interdependence means that no member can function without the others. And the members, individually or collectively, cannot function without Christ.

I learned early in my Christian experience what it means to be a part of the body of Christ. My family had not attended church in a number of years, not since I was in about the third grade. As a teenager, I was invited by some of my girl friends to visit their Sunday School class. I went, liked it, and continued.

Slowly I began to feel like a part of the group, to be accepted. I had always—for a number of reasons—felt different from the other boys and girls my age. In this church I still had a sense of being different, but it no longer seemed to matter so much. About a year after starting to attend church, I was converted.

A year or two later—when I was seventeen or eighteen—I was recruited ("drafted" is probably a better word) to work with the first- and second-grade children in Sunday School. I knew nothing about such work. But in a small-town church no one asks you if you can do the job. They just put you in it and let you learn!

As I worked with those children, I began to get a sense of my gifts. I was a good storyteller. I enjoyed the Bible and wanted to make it real to these children.

Still later I became the president of our Youth group. I had never thought of myself in a leadership position. Again, my importance as a part of the body of Christ was being affirmed. I would never have thought of myself as having gifts or as being a working part of the body. But other people saw in me what I did not see in myself. I am sure that I would never have moved into places of leadership that I have since held without the faith of other members of the church in an awkward, shy, eager, young Christian.

The Church as the Family of God

The extended family was very important in New Testament times. Loss of family relationships was considered a tragedy. Jesus warned that one of the painful consequences of following him would be a loss of family (Matt. 10:34-36). The family of God restored lost family relationships and expanded them to include all those who belonged to Christ. For those who came into the church as families, they were given many more persons to relate to.

There are four important characteristics of the family of God: interrelatedness, equality under the head of the family, a shared history and shared value system, and mutual concern and mutual support.

In patriarchal families, there was a head of the extended family (which included a number of related families). This was the father or the oldest male member. The family members were secure in being related to one another. They might be disapproved, but they still belonged to the family. And with one head, the members could be free to relate to each other in equality, knowing that the head carried the family's authority.

Shared history and shared values are important in a family. A shared history means that there is understanding among the members. Shared values means that everyone knows what is accepted or not accepted within the extended family.

In a family, there are mutual concern and mutual support. One problem with our fragmented families today is that we do not have enough relatives to turn to in times of need. Aunts, uncles, cousins, brothers and sisters, parents and grandparents all may live at great distances from one another. But an extended family that lives close together gives mutual support.

The church provides a place where all the generations can

meet as one family. It is probably the major institution where children, youth, adults, old people, men, women, married, widowed, divorced, and never married can meet together. In the church, there is a recognition of the relatedness of all the members. There is a family feeling. Not everyone may share this feeling, but it is there.

Further, there is equality among the members under one Father. Each member is an important part of the family. No one has the right to pull rank on another or to set himself or herself up as the authority in the family of God. (This includes the ministers of the church, as well as the lay members.) The Father's will is to be the most important consideration of all the members. Jesus' words, "Seek ye first the kingdom of God," indicate the priority for the family of God. Just as all the family members work together in the family business, all the church members must work together for the kingdom of their Father.

The church does have a shared history and shared values. "Salvation history" is the term used for what God has been doing with and for human beings since the beginning of time. So the family of God has a long history to share. Different denominations and churches can add their own histories to the sharing. The family of God has a definite value system to share. The Bible clearly states the values by which the family of God is to operate.

Mutual concern and mutual support are strong characteristics of the family of God. Just as one looks to one's family for support, one can look to the family of God for help in time of trouble.

I remember when my father died, at midnight on a Good Friday. My mother and I were all the family. Aunts, uncles, and cousins were in far distant places. The doctor who came to the house to confirm that my father had died was concerned that I had no brothers or sisters to turn to. But I told him that I had plenty of help available.

The next morning I called a Christian couple who were my good friends—and who had both lost their fathers. Within minutes they were at my house. The man helped me make all the funeral and burial arrangements. The woman stayed with Mother, made telephone calls to many people, contacted pall-bearers, and arranged for food. Mutual concern and mutual support were all around me. My Christian friends came swarming to help. In fact, we ran out of things for people to do! No member of the family of God needs to face the crises of life alone.

The Church as the Caring Community

Just as the body provides for the nourishment and growth of its members, so the church provides for its members. Just as a family provides fellowship and mutual support for its members, so does the church. It is also the medium through which many of the resources of God are passed on to his children.

The worth of the individual and the diversity of gifts can be lived out in the church. There is a place for every person's gifts, and those gifts are needed if the church is to thrive.

This is also the place to nourish relationships between persons. A good gardener does not plant his best seeds out in the ground, to let them be buffeted by wind, rain, and cold when they are young. Rather, he plants them in a protected place, such as a greenhouse or seedbed. Then, when they have become able to withstand the weather, he puts them into the garden.

Most people, especially lonely people, have difficulty relating to persons with whom they do not feel comfortable. This is one reason persons shrink from relationships: it is painful to be rejected. But the church provides a climate of love and acceptance. God's love through Christ pervades the church. In the sunlight of that love, it is easier to risk loving other people. And when one has a firm base of friends within the church, it is easier to risk relationships with persons who may not be so accepting at first.

Also, the church is the temple of the Holy Spirit (Eph. 2:21-22). Just as the Spirit dwells in individuals, he dwells in the church as a whole. His guidance and encouragement can be powerfully felt when the church is following his leadership.

In the church, the fruits of the Spirit ripen. Many of these qualities relate to personal interactions. They cannot be developed in isolation. As church members interact with one another, the Spirit works to grow his fruit in his people.

Of course, no church will act like the body of Christ and the family of God all the time. Nor will any church always act so that the resources of God can be mediated through it. As has been said earlier, the church is human as well as divine. Its faults are clear for all to see. But in almost every church, or in sections of every church, there will be found characteristics of the family of God and the body of Christ. God will see that his resources are made available through the church in one form or another.

For this reason it is important for lonely persons to look carefully for a church home. The best church for a lonely person is where he can get important relational and personal needs met. The closest church may not be the best one. A church farther away, but with diverse ministries, may provide more resources. But the neighborhood church may be just the right one for a family seeking friends in their own community.

Also, it is important to remember that every church has in it many lonely persons, as well as many caring persons. Lonely persons are in the church trying to get their needs met. They may not yet be at the stage where they can help other persons. If you are a lonely person yourself, you may find little fellowship with these people.

One day I sat in a Sunday School planning conference. A group of singles were discussing their efforts to bring more people into their class. They seemed to be at a loss to understand what they were doing wrong or what they needed to do differently in order to attract new members.

Finally one very shy woman spoke up. "I'll tell you one thing," she said quietly. "I've been coming to this Sunday School class for about a year off and on. When I'm not there, no one calls to ask me why I haven't come. And when I do come, I don't feel welcome. Nobody asks me where I've been or seems glad to see me."

The reaction of the Sunday School class was revealing. All of the members turned on the woman. They began to blame her for not letting them know of her needs. They asked her why she had waited so long to tell them this. Not one word was said about how the class needed to change its actions and attitudes. The people in the class, as I knew, were lonely people. They were still tied up with their own worries and fears about being alone. They were not able to hear the cry for help from this member.

It is not surprising that a short time later the woman left the class altogether. Within a few months she had joined a Sunday School class in another church.

Still, in the local church and its programs, the body of Christ and the family of God are seen. I want to set out the various activities of the church and show how they are—or can be—expressive of the body of Christ and the family of God. If you are a lonely person, you can use these activities as a checklist to help you relate to a church where your needs can be met. And persons in the church can gain from these pages insights into ways to make their church more of what God intends it to be.

The major expression of the church is always the Sunday morning worship service. It attracts the largest crowds. The service embodies most of the spiritual elements of worship, instruction, inspiration, and fellowship that are characteristic of the church. Many people do not take advantage of these elements as they should. Nor do they use the time to build fellowship with others in the service. But they can.

Here in one spot are gathered all the diverse members of the body of Christ: the old and the young, the men and the women, the single and the married. High and low, rich and poor, all are equal at the foot of the cross. No one needs to feel out of place. The purpose is the worship of God, and he calls on all human beings to worship him. So everyone belongs here.

The parts of the service are designed to help people worship God: through praise, confession of sin, acceptance of forgiveness, consecration of life, and growth in understanding God's will. All these things can be done in solitude. But when they are done in a group of people, they are enhanced. My praise of God in song is magnified if I hear many other voices raised with mine. My confession of sin is less painful if I know that others are doing the same thing. Any decision I make—to become a Christian, to join the church, to consecrate myself more fully to God's will—is strengthened when my Christian brothers and sisters affirm that decision by their support.

Even giving seems a happier experience when many people share in it. Some churches have the custom of presenting special offerings or pledges in a worship service. Again, the gift is enhanced when we know that many others are joining with us.

So the worship service on Sunday morning is a great support for those who are lonely. Even when you do not know anyone in church, you know that these are your people. Everyone is present for the same purpose. Everyone shares in the same experiences. Everyone can move out of the service closer to each other.

This closeness is not always evident after a worship service. People are preoccupied, in a hurry to get to a restaurant or to meet another engagement. But if you feel that you are on the outside, remember that these people's spiritual oneness is more apt to be evident in smaller, more informal groups.

Sunday School Classes

A Sunday School, or Bible study, class is probably the best place for a lonely person to begin to make friends in the church. This class should be small enough for persons to learn to know each other—about ten to twenty-five members. The group should be of similar age and experiences, so that persons can relate to one another more easily. It is also important to learn to know people who are different. But that should come after a base of friendship has been established. It is better to have friends on whom you can rely before starting to look for friends where your overtures may be rebuffed. Then, if such rebuffs come, you will be able to turn to the friends you already have.

The Sunday School class should engage in authentic Bible study. By this I mean a study of the Bible that is not superficial. Simply rehashing the lesson material or "reading a verse around" does not fill the needs of persons for a growing understanding of God's Word.

In authentic Bible study, the teacher leads the class to an understanding of the Bible material and in a discussion of the relevance of the biblical truths for everyday living. In such an atmosphere, persons can learn to share with one another. Problems and concerns of everyday life can be shared in the light of what God's Word has to say about Christian living.

Think of a study of Jesus' words on Christian economics in Matthew 6:25-33. The biblical truths relate to putting God's kingdom first and not allowing material problems to be paramount in the Christian's life. These truths relate immediately to everyday life. Class members may discuss various problems they have with budgets, moonlighting, or putting children through school. They may go further and talk about the strain that economic problems place on marriages. Or they may share their worries about caring for aged parents on a limited income.

A Bible study that is authentic makes it possible for the members to share at whatever level they feel comfortable with one another. As groups continue to meet together, they can talk at deeper levels. Such conversation opens the door for true friendships.

A Sunday School class is also a caring group. It is the place where there can be a sensitive awareness of the lives of other persons. When each person is aware of the presence and value of other persons in the group, there is the opportunity for real communication. Where a group is banded together to learn what the Bible says and how it applies to their lives, they are more ready to be sensitive to others. They are not thinking only of themselves.

The church is under obligation from God the Father to accept all his children, even the most unlovely and the most unloving. In the church people can come into the worship service, prayer meeting, or Sunday School class and know that they will not be thrown out. In the church persons can hope to share a bond of trust in a community where people care for one another. That hope comes alive most clearly in a small group like a Sunday School class.

Most classes which care about their members are organized to make such caring actual. Some classes divide the members into smaller groups, with persons assigned to care for the individuals in the groups. These classes are always aware of needs among the members: sickness, changes in the family, deaths, other concerns. Prayers for the sick and sharing of information are a part of the class session. In such a climate, a lonely person can begin to feel accepted and wanted.

The Sunday School class helps to build up the body of Christ. The ingredients which the body needs to stay alive, humanly speaking, are air, water, food, shelter, exercise, rest and sleep, proper elimination, and social contacts. The body of Christ needs trust and trustworthiness, forgiveness and reconciliation, hope, and love. In the small groups, such as the Sunday School class, other study groups, prayer groups, and service groups, these elements can be practiced among the members. As they are, the whole body is strengthened. And individuals, especially lonely persons, find themselves growing in their ability to relate to others in healthy, loving ways.

Trust and trustworthiness are necessary for any kind of personal relationship. Persons and groups in the church must be able to rely on the words and deeds of each other. Each person, therefore, must be trustworthy. Without the confidence that others will sustain the person, rather than betray him or her, there can be no community. Of course, in the presence of trustworthiness, the person must learn to lean on the others. Refusing to trust persons when they have proved themselves trustworthy is one immediate way to destroy friendships.

However, the actual fact is that persons will betray one another in various ways at times. Each person is capable of breaking promises as well as keeping them. So forgiveness is needed between persons in the church. The writers of the epistles, especially Paul, were realistic in recognizing this ability to be untrustworthy. Christians in the church do not set out to betray each other. But self-interest, lack of understanding, and human weakness make it easy for persons to be untrustworthy at times. Also, some persons have expectations of others that are not spelled out. If one person expects another to do something without making the expectation clear, it is easy for the other person to fail.

Forgiveness is absolutely necessary if the church is to survive. If the broken promises and disappointments of the past remain unforgiven, these become like open wounds in the body. They will fester, become infected, and undermine the total health of the body. Love does not ignore broken relationships. Rather, it is clear about facing the breach of friendship (see Matt. 5:23-24) and doing something about it. A wound is not healed by covering it up and acting as if it did not exist.

Most disagreements and disappointments between the members begin as small wounds. But if they are not treated with loving-kindness and forgiveness, they will fester. Forgiveness by the wronged person is like treating a wound with an antibiotic: It is a specific treatment that combats the powers of infection. But love and kindness on the part of all the church members are also necessary. These are like the blood circulating, bringing healing and strength to both parties in the dispute.

When the wounds are healed, the whole body is again able to function without anything hampering it. Remember that a wound in any part of the body affects the whole body. So wounds of disagreement and loss of trust between even two members affect the whole body of Christ.

Love is another essential ingredient for the body of Christ. Love has already been defined in chapter 3. But love between members of the body of Christ is deeper in quality and power than love of neighbor. Love between neighbors requires that each person desire the welfare of the other as he desires his own welfare. But love between Jesus' disciples is the quality that would call one person to give up his or her life for the benefit of others (see John 15:12-14). This self-sacrificing love is most like God's love. Just as he gave his Son to save the lives of human beings, his disciples are to give their lives to save their brothers and sisters in Christ. Note that such self-sacrifice is not required toward persons outside of Christ. But anyone who so loves his brother and sister in Christ will have increasing ability to love all persons in the same way.

Love means more than self-giving action. It includes profound respect for others, for who they are. It celebrates the difference between persons and rejoices in what makes other persons unique. In these ways, Christian love echoes the love which God has for his highest creatures. In such love, there is neither a swallowing up of other persons (Gal. 5:15) nor a blind submission to others. Love maintains distance between persons even while it gratefully acknowledges dependence between persons.

Hope, another life-support element, is built on faith. It looks toward the future, both for humankind and for the church. Hope believes that the future is not fixed in such a way that statisticians can make firm predictions about it. Christian hope recognizes that at any moment God can and will break into history to make unpredicted changes. Human beings, also, are capable of such unpredictable behavior.

Hope relates to the freedom to change. In this way, it is tied to personal freedom. The more freedom persons have for their lives and the more responsibility they accept for their conduct, the stronger is the possibility of creative change. This is what the church is about. It is a change-agent. Therefore it deals in hope. If persons, through the grace of God, can change, it is the work of the church to set up a climate in which such changes can come about. "Thy kingdom come. Thy will be done in earth, as it is in heaven," is a profoundly hopeful prayer. If it were not possible for the kingdom to come on earth and for God's will to be done within the limits of time and space, this would be a cynical prayer!

All these elements are best experienced in the small groups that are so much a part of every church. Because we tend to think of the church as being embodied in the morning worship service, we may tend to discount the small groups. But they are vital to the church. Without their life-giving activities, no church would survive long.

Other Small Groups

Sunday School classes are the first line of small groups in the church. But there are many others. Every small group in the church offers the possibility of relationships. No matter what the purpose of the group, a hidden but real purpose is for people to get together.

However, the healthiest groups do not major purely on social functions. The group that centers on itself and its social needs will gradually deteriorate. Groups that meet for service, for inspiration, for learning—with social needs as an important secondary purpose—generally thrive.

Service groups help to meet the needs of the body of Christ for exercise. Just as no body grows strong without using its muscles, no church can be strong without serving others. Lonely people can find their own spiritual muscles growing, also, as they work in service groups. And sharing in tasks enhances fellowship among the workers.

Some of the service groups in churches are missionary groups, evangelistic groups, committees and boards of the church, and community service groups.

Learning or inspiration groups include prayer meeting, small prayer groups, weekday Bible study groups, book clubs, and other groups that meet on Sunday night or during the week for study of various kinds. Choirs and instrumental groups are both learning and service groups. Many people who are tongue-tied around other persons can express themselves in music groups. In this way, they can grow to the point that they can make friends among their fellow musicians. From there they can go on to wider ranges of fellowship within the church.

In talking so much about the small groups in the church, it is not my intention to suggest that lonely people should find friends only there. But given the family feeling of the church, this is the best place to start building relationships.

Groups in the church are well suited to help persons meet social needs which are often frustrated in our competitive individualistic society. These needs are:

(1) For community—the ability to live in trust and cooperation with others in a caring group.

(2) For opportunities to share differing views with other persons in a climate of safety and acceptance.

(3) For a chance to be dependent. We all want a community where we can allow ourselves to be weak, to show that we need others. There is strength in shared dependence. Everyone has a strength which is not shared by all the others. So each person can lend strength to the group and draw strength from the group.

(4) For in-depth sharing. This is more than sharing differing views. This involves a contract between persons whereby each person is allowed to be himself or herself, to be free to make mistakes and still feel assured that he or she will not be cut off from others. The contract involves trust, forgiveness, love, and hope, as outlined earlier in this chapter.

Without such sharing, there are no deep friendships. The small groups in the church offer a healthy climate for learning to share in depth with others. And as persons share deeply, the whole body is strengthened. Where there is little or no open sharing, there are barriers between persons. Each such barrier that is raised drives persons back into isolation and into loneliness. It is not possible to share deeply with everyone; nor is it advisable. But everyone needs a few persons with whom to share as one would with a close family member—a brother or sister, a father or mother. So sharing builds the family feeling as well.

Family Ties in the Church

The whole church, as the caring community, provides such family ties between persons. These ties may exist within a specific congregation. They may be found wherever Christians become friends. And they may be seen whenever two strangers who are Christians encounter each other.

It is unfortunate that we do not have the signal system that the early Christians used to contact each other. In the days of persecution, the Christians would use the sign of the fish. They would trace in the dirt, with toe, stick, or finger, two curving lines crossing each other in roughly the shape of a fish. These lines also were the way the Greeks made the capital letter Chi, the first letter of the name of Christ. When two persons met, the shared symbol of the fish marked them as disciples of Christ.

But Christians today have ways of signaling each other. A Bible, religious jewelry, a bumper sticker, or the mention of a church can be a symbol that one is a Christian.

I saw this dramatically portrayed twice on a business trip. Three of us, all religious workers, were sitting in a hotel lobby late one night sharing some of our Christian experiences. A hotel porter, on late night duty, was sitting nearby where he could hear us. After a while, he left the room. He returned shortly, carrying a Bible. He sat down nearby, opened the Bible, and began to read it. He held the book where we could easily see what it was. When we rose to leave, we saw his signal. For a few moments we visited with him and shared our faith together.

Later on the same trip we three were in an airport terminal. Again we were sharing with one another. A man sitting across from us reached into his pocket and pulled out a church bulletin. He held it up where we could see it. We caught his signal and included him in our conversation.

The church would do well to find ways by which Christians can communicate with one another more easily. As has been said earlier, the church is not confined to any one congregation. Rich experiences come to the person who reaches out to find Christian friends in many other places.

This attachment between persons in the family of God is like attachment in a family. People do not have to achieve something or be perfect in order to belong in a family. What ties the family together are the desires to love and be loved; to be needed; to be secure; and to belong to the group. Where these feelings are sensed and these needs are met, there is a "consciousness of kind." In a family, this term means that persons of a shared name and family history are somehow different from persons with different names and a different history. Christians have a shared name and a shared family history. They also have a shared purpose in living.

But this consciousness of kind, if it becomes exclusive can be a threat to the family of God and the body of Christ. The family must be constantly expanding. The body must be constantly renewing itself, as members die. So the church's main mission is to bring other persons into the caring community. This means relating to different people, those who are far from God. Where consciousness of kind is too strong, members of the church may shrink from these different persons.

A church I know about had a very strong family feeling. The people loved each other and related warmly to one another. But they were too exclusive. They really were not interested in bringing other persons into the church. One woman summed up the church's attitude by saying, "I know that we ought to be concerned about getting other people to join the church. But I love our church just the way it is. I don't want it to get so big that I won't know everyone in it. I just wish it could stay the same way forever."

But a living body does not stay "the same way forever." There are changes, toward life or toward death. That church, through the years, has declined in membership as well as in active concern for outsiders. It is not the same church it was several years ago. It is a fine body—but a weaker one.

Family Celebrations in the Church

Like any other family, the church has many family celebrations which serve to build community. Lonely people, wanting to be a part of that community, need to involve themselves deeply in these special celebrations. Churches need to increase such family times. These special events not only build community but also they encourage other people to want to be a part of this caring community.

Throughout the year the church has many opportunities for celebration. Christmas and Easter are probably the most important times for many churches. There are also New Year's, Lent, Pentecost, Thanksgiving, Memorial Day, Mother's Day, and Father's Day. Some churches make special events of Independence Day, Labor Day, and graduation.

Churches with a strong sense of family develop especially meaningful holiday celebrations. A church to which I used to belong established an early morning praise-and-testimony service for Thanksgiving. The worshipers gathered about 7:00 AM. After a brief worship time, the meeting was thrown open for anyone to share a testimony, ask for a hymn of praise to be sung, call for a psalm to be read, or lead in prayer. Member after member would rise to remember some time of blessing or crisis during the past year and to thank God for his goodness. As persons were members over a period of years, they learned to know and share with one another more deeply. There never was a service where tears of joy or sorrow were not shed.

In my own church, we celebrate Thanksgiving with a turkey dinner on Wednesday night. This is followed by the celebration of the Lord's Supper around the tables.

The weeks leading up to Christmas are really family time for many churches, especially those which celebrate Advent. The Advent wreath is lit each Sunday. Carols are sung. Christmas decorations, including Christian symbols, are hung. Special activities of care for others are included.

In one church all the members join in intergenerational groups on one Sunday evening before Christmas. They prepare baskets of fruit and cookies and then, still in the cross-generational groups, take these to shut-in members of the church. Other churches have special carol sings, either for the benefit of some charitable group or simply for the joy of singing to people.

Memorial Day is a time for remembering the members of the congregation who have died. Mother's Day—and sometimes

Father's Day—can be a time of celebrating new life born into the congregation.

Some churches make special events of high school and college graduation, letting the young people know how important their academic achievements are in the life of the church. And other churches have Fourth of July picnics, summer ice-cream festivals, or summer camp experiences that enhance family feeling. No one ever needs to bewail the lack of family reunions if he or she belongs to such a church.

Note

1. Fort Worth *Star-Telegram* quoting column by Marjorie Hyer ©1980 *The Washington Post*, August 16, 1980.

5

Learn to Believe
You Are Worth Caring About

Elissa is a married woman with two school age children. She has a job in a small company which permits her to be at home when the children arrive from school. She desperately wants friends among the people she works with. She has tried everything, she thinks—sitting with people at coffee break, inviting a co-worker to lunch with her, chatting casually with people during the work day. But nothing works.

She does not recognize the real cause of her lack of friends. Whenever she is with someone else, she begins to complain about the problems in her life. If anyone praises her, she goes into detail about her inadequacies. Often she will be too aggressive in her attempts to make friends, abruptly inviting herself to a table where others are having a private conversation. Or she may issue an invitation to lunch in such a way that the person cannot refuse. She talks a great deal about herself. But if the other person begins to share and invites a similar confidence, she withdraws immediately.

Such actions betray personal attitudes that keep people from friendships. These attitudes are a sense of personal unworthiness and a fear of really getting close to another person, except someone already in the family.

Personal causes of loneliness are rooted in childhood conditioning. The child may feel unworthy to have friends. He or she may not feel permission to make friends outside of home and relatives. Such conditioning is almost always unconscious and is hardly ever deliberate. Parents are human, and they make mistakes in child rearing. They may pass on to their children their own unhealthy patterns of relating. Often such patterns are repeated generation after generation.

The child also may pick up wrong ideas from the parents. From the limited perspective of a small individual, it is easy to suppose that parental reprimands of "dumb, silly, and ugly" mean that the person—not just the child's actions—is character- ized by these adjectives. So a child grows up to think of himself or herself as dumb, silly, or ugly.

But just as the child picks up ideas in childhood that steer his course in later life, he can change those ideas. A person is the most adaptable of God's creatures. In the home the child adapts in order to get along with parents, brothers, and sisters. But the same adaptability that got the child into loneliness patterns can get the adult out of them!

The first thing that needs to be changed is the view of self. A person with a poor self-image cannot attract friends. Nor can she build up strength for relationships when self-esteem is very low.

At this point it would be good to reread what is said about the worth of the individual in chapter 3. Without a firm basis outside oneself on which to build self-worth, all the psychologi- cal exercises in the world will not make a real difference. Fix in your mind the fact that God loves you for your uniqueness. Re- alize that it is his will for you to be yourself, not somebody else.

Now begin to change your old habits of thinking about yourself. Perhaps without realizing it, are you constantly putting yourself down? Whenever you make a mistake, do you call yourself "dumb" or "silly"? Do you scold yourself for every error? If so, your attitude toward yourself is that of a harsh authority figure. You will constantly find things to blame in yourself and seldom anything to praise.

Begin to allow yourself to hear these internal messages and

to be very aware of them. Notice how often they occur during the course of a day.

After you have become really aware of your inner self-belittling, begin to change these messages. Find a statement that expresses your worth and uniqueness. It may be: I am a unique and valuable person. God made me, and he never makes trash; so I am valuable. God loves me enough that he gave his Son for me. I am worth being someone's friend. I am special, just as I am.

Choose one of these statements or formulate your own. Be sure it is one that strongly expresses worth. Repeat it to yourself several times. You will have contradictory feelings about this statement. You will feel good about it, but you will also feel uncomfortable. It goes against what you have been saying about yourself for many years. So it will be hard to believe or to say. But say it anyway!

Write out your statement. Tape it on the mirror in the bathroom, on the refrigerator door, or on the visor in the car. Put a copy in your wallet. It should be in places where you can see it and be reminded of its message.

Then decide on at least three specific times a day when you will repeat this statement five times to yourself. (That is a total of fifteen times a day.) Choose times when you will be sure to remember. These may be when shaving or putting on makeup, starting out to work, or drinking a second cup of coffee at mid-morning.

Even though you intend to do so, you will not always remember at these times. Don't be angry with yourself when this happens. It takes a long time to form new habits. The old ways feel comfortable, like an old shoe. You can slip into them as you do into the old shoe, without feeling pressure. A new habit, like a new shoe, can pinch! Keep telling yourself, however, that building self-esteem is important for your well-being. Also, as you build this new habit, you are developing your ability to change. You will need this skill as you tackle other problems that keep you from making friends.

Beginning to enhance your self-esteem is the first step. Next comes the recognition that love and friendship are available to all human beings. The myth that friendships are scarce is deeply rooted in our competitive society. We get the idea that only in the family can one find total acceptance and love. So persons cling to their nuclear families. Or they hasten to get married in the hope that the mate will supply all their emotional needs.

Many persons cling to the family-love myth tenaciously. A man in a singles group was bemoaning the fact that all of his immediate family had died, and now other relatives were dying. "I have no one at all to talk to," he said.

One of the women in the group said to him, "You can talk to me. I'll be glad for you to call me anytime you feel blue and lonesome."

He looked at her almost in horror. "I wouldn't think of doing that!" he replied.

Of course he wouldn't. That kind of thinking was foreign to him. He had never let himself think of getting acceptance and warmth beyond his family circle.

Like this man, we program ourselves for what we get. If we believe that we can get only a few friends, that is what we plan and work for. We can create scarcity where there is no lack.

My mother was like that about water. She grew up in a small town where the water supply came from private wells and cisterns. Her family had to carry water a long way in order to water the stock. Even in very cold weather they had to pump water from the outside well for their needs.

Late in her life my mother moved to a city. Here water was not only plentiful but also there was a minimum charge whether the water was used or not. It was advisable to use the water for which you had paid.

But my mother's mind was so set that she could not change her thinking about water. She continued to wash her hands in a small amount of water. She preferred sponge baths to the tub. Anyone who used water in any quantity became the object of her anger. She was constantly afraid that the family would run out of water.

This is the way many lonely people react to love and friendship. They are so afraid that there will not be enough to go around that they hoard the friendships they have. They want only a few good friends. They find even these hard to cultivate. This reinforces their belief that friendship is a scarce commodity.

If you have such a belief, start now to change it. Begin by recognizing that "God is love." Since this is true, love is inexhaustible because God is limitless. There will always be enough for everyone. The more love we give, the more it is possible for us to receive.

At this point you may find yourself resisting. Why should you shrink away from love and acceptance if this is what you want? Perhaps you have a fear of being close to someone else. This fear may have come from childhood conditioning. You may have had parents who did not know how to give warmth and were afraid of it. Think back into your childhood. What kinds of friends did your family have? How did your parents show that they loved you? Did you get a lot of hugging and kissing or very little? Did your parents show affection to each other?

If you have a background of being distant, you cannot change that overnight. To try to would be disastrous. You would run as fast as you could from the closeness you desire and yet fear. Instead, begin by having friends and getting personal contacts where you will not have to fear getting close.

A psychiatrist whom I know made a study of the personal contacts which are needed for persons to be emotionally healthy. (Recall the study by Spitz referred to in chapter 2.) He divided these contacts among those given to oneself, those given by close family and friends, and those given by all others. His findings were amazing. They contradict much of what we believe about the scarcity of love and acceptance. He said that, of 100 percent of such contacts, a healthy person will get 25 percent from himself or herself, 20 percent from close family and friends, and 55 percent from all others.

If it were not possible for us to get personal contacts in all of these ways, such a ratio would be not only unrealistic but also unkind. There is love all around us. You have only to open yourself to it, as the flower opens to the sun and the rain. A smile from a little child, a friendly word from a store clerk, a wave from a neighbor are personal contacts that build up our store of acceptance. All too many people ignore or reject these contacts, but they go to make up the total.

It is like building up a savings account. Some people wait to make a deposit until they get a thousand-dollar check. But wiser people keep putting in the little amounts they receive day by day—fifty cents, a dollar, ten dollars. You don't have to wait to spend a whole evening with a loved one in order to fill up your "bank account." You can cherish every personal contact that comes your way.

Your internal "personal contacts" help to build the bank account also. Giving yourself statements about your personal worth, as suggested earlier in this chapter, is a way of building self-esteem. The more good things you say to yourself, the more you will like yourself. And the more you will find to say!

A cartoon, "The Dumplings," in the mid-1970s, showed how ordinary people could really find themselves special. In one cartoon the man is saying: "I'm a lucky guy . . . I make enough to get by on . . . I got a li'l gal who's nuts about me . . . and not only that, but I'm good-lookin'." Because he felt good about himself, he could enjoy his blessings of work and love without hesitation. The better you feel about yourself, the more you will be able to celebrate your blessings and say good things to yourself.

A good way to build up your bank account of warmth and acceptance is to recycle your personal contacts. You may keep a diary, a record of all the contacts that come your way during the day. You may even make a check sheet, listing these warm contacts under Self, Family, Others. In this way you can evaluate, at the end of a week, whether you are keeping the healthy ratio recommended by my psychiatrist friend.

One warning: Don't discount the warm contacts you get! It is easy to say, "That was just a passing glance," or "He was nice to me because he was paid to be." Take the warm contact and enjoy it!

At the same time, you are free to refuse contacts about which you genuinely feel uncomfortable. If a man leers at a woman, she doesn't have to smile if she doesn't enjoy it. If a woman leans all over a man, he doesn't have to respond if he doesn't want to. But these contacts are the minority. The more good contacts you open yourself to, the less vulnerable you will be to persons who want to manipulate you by their attentions.

The best personal contacts are—as they were in babyhood —the "touching" ones. Again we have a theory of scarcity to contend with. We believe that one should not hug, kiss, or touch another person warmly unless related to that person by blood or marriage. But this is another myth. The early Christians spoke often of greeting one another with "a holy kiss." The kiss was no less real because it was holy! The expression meant that this kind of kiss was not to be erotic. It was to indicate the deep love the Christians had for one another.

Since most of us are so far separated from our families, we need more outlets for warm touches. It would be a good idea to develop a number of "kissing cousins" among our friends. This can happen in the family atmosphere of the church. I find that when I am feeling warm and accepting, I get a lot of touching at church. I can get a basketful of hugs, smiles, pats, and a kiss or two as I walk the length of our fellowship hall.

Childhood conditioning also is involved in our attitudes toward other people and the possibilities of friendship. Persons set up barriers to friendship within their own heads.

A woman called me one day to discuss a workshop I was planning to lead. She said that she wanted to come so that she could make new friends. But in the next breath she began a long tirade about how difficult—even impossible—it was to make friends in Fort Worth.

"This is the most unfriendly town I've ever lived in," she said. "Nobody wants to be your friend. I don't have any money, and so people aren't interested in me. I'm unemployed just now. I can't afford to get the grass cut, and nobody is going to come to my house and walk through that front yard. And my house isn't nicely decorated because I can't afford it. So I know nobody wants to come here."

As I listened to her reasons—delivered in rapid-fire fashion —I thought I could tell her some other reasons why she was having trouble making friends. But she wasn't interested in hearing any other reasons, and I knew that. She wanted to see herself as a victim of outward circumstances. Then she could justify her lack of friends.

I would have needed several conversations with her in order to discover the personal reasons for her lack of friends. But I could hazard one guess: Those reasons were rooted in her childhood. Somewhere she had picked up the idea that friendship and economics were connected. If you have enough money, a good job, and the right surroundings, you can have friends. Otherwise—forget it! I could imagine her parents saying, "Those people down the street are snobs. They don't want to associate with us. Look at that fine car. We'll just stay away from them."

Hearing statements like that throughout childhood can set up alarm systems within the growing person. These alarm systems are kept internally and can be activated whenever a situation seems to hold potential danger or discomfort. Since these alarm systems were set early in childhood, they may not be appropriate now. But like the woman with her economic mind set, they are often not questioned.

Consider these alarms. How many of them do you hear in your own head when you consider venturing out to make friends?

We don't belong. People don't want us. We stay with our own kind: All warnings to keep the child from making new and different friends.

Don't get close. It's dangerous to be close to people unless they are related. Don't share with anyone but your spouse or your close family: All warnings to keep the child isolated from others.

You'll never make it: A warning against taking a risk in relationships (or anything else). If you're not going to succeed, why get started at all?

You need to be different. You should have been a boy (or a girl). You're not worth anything the way you are: All warnings that the person cannot hope to be anybody so long as he or she insists on remaining the same person.

This is the bad news: We carry about with us old baggage that gets in the way of our having good relationships. There are other destructive or warning internal messages, also. If you listen carefully to what goes on inside your head, you'll be bound to hear them.

But this is the good news: You can change the old messages and deactivate the outmoded alarm systems. You can use the same type of control that was suggested in building self-esteem. It is a matter of learning new habits while you unlearn old ones. Here are the steps to follow:

(1) Recognize that the ideas which are keeping you from developing relationships are not realistic. It is easy to see that the

woman on the telephone had unrealistic ideas. It may be harder to see that your old ideas are likewise unrealistic. They are based on your family's circumstances. There might have been good reasons for your parents to react toward relationships as they did. But their circumstances are not yours. You live in a different time and place. You can develop your life to fit your circumstances.

(2) Begin to change the alarm systems in your head. When you find yourself parroting some old idea, stop and examine it. Is this true of you now? Is this the way you want to live? When you reply no to these questions, give yourself permission to change the old message to a new one. Instead of, "We don't belong," say to yourself, "I can belong." Instead of saying, "It's dangerous to get close," say, "It's natural to get close." Instead of, "You can't make it," say, "Yes, I can make it!" Instead of, "Be different," say, "I have the right and obligation to be who I am."

(3) Realize that getting rid of these old alarm systems is going to be uncomfortable at first. If for years you had carried a gun every time you went outdoors, it would take a long time for you to feel comfortable if you went without one. But if the circumstances don't warrant carrying a gun, it's time to get rid of it. That is the situation with you as a grown-up person. You no longer need the childhood fears and cautions that helped to protect you from the outside world.

In addition to your conditioning toward relationships, there is also the general attitude toward life engendered by the way you were reared. All of us have some unhealthy spots in our personalities. These are our responses to the way our parents dealt with us as children. Certain symptoms that appear in clusters might be called syndromes, as the physician describes the symptoms of scarlet fever or muscular dystrophy. Each person has his or her share of these syndromes; some people have more, some less. Usually these spots appear in combination in the personality. When they are present to any degree, they affect adversely the person's ability to function as an adult.

As you read the following syndromes, decide which ones fit for you. See whether they are limiting your effectiveness in dealing with other persons. Use the "antidotes" to become more mature and thus better able to relate to others.

(1) The Push-Pull Syndrome.—This person can't get started at a task, no matter how important it is. The person is always saying internally, "Should, ought, need to, must, have to." But the push-pull comes in always putting off the time when these internal orders will be carried out. This person harbors the hidden feeling that doing such things will make little real difference anyway. The push-pull is a *push* to do something and a *pull* away from it. Even though the person knows rationally that doing certain things would be good for him, there is an emotional pull back.

These people seldom get into groups or move out to try to make friends. They get exhausted as they experience push-pull; so they do not have the energy to try. They do not consider themselves failures because they are always making resolutions about what they will do. But they never become successes because they are always stopping themselves.

They assume that doing anything will take more effort than they can put out. If they do make an attempt at friendship, it is always too much. A party becomes a major undertaking. Having a few people in can never be done lightly. The effort at social life always seems to take more out of these people than it does others. So, if such effort is required, the person must resist. But the individual does not realize that the demands are of his or her own making.

Antidote: Stop saying "should, ought, or have to." Substitute "can, want to, have decided to, am going to, and will." Instead of saying, "I have to go out and make friends," say, "I can go out and make friends." Such words change the internal climate. Instead of your emotions, mind, and even your muscles tightening up over the prospect of a new venture, the other words will give you a feeling of relaxation and confidence. You will need to say the words over and over because they will not feel comfortable to you at first. You will not believe them. But say them anyway!

Also, set realistic goals for yourself. Instead of planning a dinner party for eight, plan a luncheon for four. Instead of planning a date that includes dinner and the symphony, begin with a simple invitation to meet for a Coke. Your inner "push-pull" thrives by making you feel that what you attempt cannot possibly be done. It magnifies whatever you plan to do by giving you the impression it will take too much effort.

To combat this impression, rationally figure out how much time and effort a realistic plan—such as the luncheon—will take. In my push-pull days, I often had trouble doing so simple a task as washing dishes. I would imagine that it would take an hour to do the dishes. But the fact was that it took about twenty minutes, even for a large amount of dishes.

Another help in overcoming the fear of getting started is not to focus on the effort, but on the outcome. Instead of thinking so much about the effort involved in a luncheon, or going with a friend to a ball game, picture the pleasure of accomplishing these friendship ventures. Concentrate on the pleasure. Minimize the effort which your mind continually dredges up.

When you have had a success, such as a luncheon or a date, allow yourself to celebrate that. Congratulate yourself on what you have done. Relive the pleasurable moments. Then make plans to repeat the pleasure by attempting another act of friendship.

(2) The Just-Perfect Syndrome.—A person afflicted with this syndrome constantly seeks to do better, to be just perfect. He or she refuses to accept less than perfection of himself or herself. Such a person will not tolerate any satisfaction over past

achievements. Always the inner refrain rings: "You could have done better. You should have been just perfect."

This person is constantly belittling himself or herself. The internal message is always: "You're not good enough. You will never do it right. You will never measure up."

Such a person cannot accept praise from others. He or she says internally that this person is prejudiced or doesn't know the facts or is just being kind. So the just perfect person discounts the other person's judgment, discrimination, and honesty.

Lonely people with this syndrome cannot believe that anyone would really like them for themselves. How could anyone, when they don't like themselves?

Antidote: Follow the instructions given earlier in this chapter for building self-esteem. As you follow these exercises, avoid the trap of blaming yourself for not doing them just perfect!

Another way to overcome self-belittlement is to listen carefully to the good things people say to you. Probably you do not hear clearly what they say. As soon as they start to speak, your internal "record player" clicks on. It is saying, "That can't be true. She is just being kind. If she only knew!"

When people begin to compliment you, force yourself to listen totally. Don't allow yourself to listen to the internal old record. Drink in the good words, as you would drink fresh water if you were thirsty. (And you are thirsty for warmth, acceptance, and praise.) When the person has finished, say simply, "Thank you. I appreciate what you have to say." Afterward repeat to yourself your friend's words. Believe what your friend said! Or at least begin to act as if you believed.

A friend of mine did this several years ago with very happy results. A never-married young man, he felt very isolated from people. He complained that no matter how he tried he could not make friends. He was afflicted with the just-perfect syndrome.

One night he was telling me of some comments that people

around him had made the night before. They had complimented his acting ability (he was in a little theater). They had told him how much fun he was when he was letting himself go.

I asked him what he thought of these comments.

"Oh, they didn't mean them," he replied. "They were just being nice. They don't believe that."

"Suppose they did," I persisted. "How would you feel?"

"Why, that would make all the difference in the world!"

Then I challenged him: "I dare you, for the rest of the show, to act as if what they are saying is so. Instead of immediately discounting what they say, allow yourself to believe it—just for the run of the show."

This challenge intrigued him. "What have I got to lose?" he laughingly agreed.

He did not call me again until the show was over. When he did, he sounded like a different person. He had begun to realize that these people did mean what they said and they did want to be his friends. As he trusted these people, he began to trust others. He gained new self-confidence. From this beginning, he went on to establish deeper relationships. Eventually he was able to make a commitment in marriage.

(3) The "Prince or Princess" Syndrome.—This person has had so many wishes granted in childhood that he or she thinks that is the way the world ought to be. This person can make friends quickly, but only on the surface. People flock to this person—at first. But as soon as some desire is not fulfilled, some wish is thwarted, the charm tends to disappear. The unstated attitude is, "If you were my friend, you'd do what I want." The prince or princess expects everyone to act as his or her parents did. As a result, few lasting friendships are formed because friendships are on the basis of give-and-take. The person is left lonely and wondering why the world is so unfeeling.

Lonely persons with this syndrome often are unhappily married, divorced, or a tyrannical marriage mate. Since he or she is a prince(ss), everyone, including a marriage partner, must bow to his or her wishes. Single persons with this syndrome may flit from one friendship or relationship to the next, never satisfied.

Antidote: Notice how many times you get your way or expect to get your way. Be stern with yourself, not making excuses or saying that your way was best. Take stock of your friendships, seeing which ones tend to evaporate over the months. Consider how much give-and-take there is in your marriage or whether things come your way most of the time.

When you have begun to be more realistic about the way you get your own wishes met, begin to look beyond yourself. When you are with another person, or in a group, concentrate on the needs and concerns of another person. It will take discipline to keep from focusing on yourself! Constantly check yourself to be sure that you are concentrating on the other person. Watch body language: hand movements, facial expression, the way the person sits or walks. Figure out what is being communicated in body language. Such exercises will keep your mind focused away from yourself.

As you are conscious of the needs of the other person, think of how you can help meet these needs. Again, this will be hard to do. It goes against the grain of your childhood conditioning. But you can do it by remembering that love is most of all concerned with the other person. That is the essence of the Golden Rule. Also, remind yourself that the prince grows up to be a king (or the princess a queen), whose main concern is to be responsible for other persons.

Offer to do something for someone else or for the group. It may be a little thing, like picking up someone or buying some of the supplies for a party. But it will give you great satisfaction. You will be spending your efforts on other people, not on yourself. And people will learn to see you, not as a spoiled brat, but as one who has something to contribute to the community.

(4) The Your-Move Syndrome.—This is the person who is so passive that he or she is always waiting for someone else to make the move. This person is often bored with life, but doesn't know what to do about it. This person would like to have friends but will not make an effort toward starting friendships. Even a slight effort in that direction is apt to be exhausting. Such a person often drifts through life, whining about the difficulties encountered.

The basis of this attitude is overindulgence on the part of the person's parents. This person's wishes were anticipated— often even before a desire was felt. Sometimes this overindulgence was a substitute for personal warmth. Parents who have never learned to give of themselves often give things instead. So the person in adulthood learns to expect special gifts and help on the part of other people as signs of their affection.

This person finds great difficulty in making friends. If he or she marries, the union is apt to be very unhappy. The person continues his or her unreasonable demands of the partner. Either the marriage ends in divorce, or the partner becomes the slave of the your-move person's expectations.

Antidote: Some persons with this syndrome have to get almost to the point of desperation before they will make any real effort to overcome loneliness. The first move, as with the prince or princess, is to recognize how much of your life is controlled by your expectations of others. For a week keep a record of the times you have waited for others to make the first move. Record the times you have missed out on opportunities to be with people because you have not wanted to make a move. Don't allow yourself to make excuses during this exercise. Simply record the facts.

After you have established your pattern, make a careful evaluation of your life-style. What would you need to change in order to be less passive? A good exercise is to take the record you have kept and mark beside each incident one thing you could have done yourself. If your inner voice tells you, "There's nothing you could have done," refuse to listen to it. If necessary, construct a fantasy in your mind of doing something to reach out to others. The main idea is to get yourself off dead center, even in your imagination.

After thinking of some things you could have done, imagine the *best possible* result. Your thinking is geared toward defeat. You need to create within yourself a climate of hope rather than despair.

The next step is to put some of these actions into practice. Choose two or three things that you will do within the next week to get you in touch with people. (Consult chapter 6 for ideas, if necessary.) Write them down so that you will remember them. No matter how difficult they seem to you, carry these out. If you find yourself becoming overly tired, recognize that this is part of your unhealthy pattern. Cut down on your expectations of yourself slightly. But force yourself to carry out at least one of the actions you decided upon.

It may take a long time to overcome your passivity. But every small success will increase your energy level! Whenever you have succeeded in making an effort, remind yourself—over and over—that you did this. Also, just as in the push-pull syndrome, remind yourself that the effort did not take as much strength as you had imagined it would. Much of what is said under push-pull applies here.

Again, recognize that there are very few pure personality types showing these syndromes. Most of us have two dominant syndromes—perhaps push-pull along with prince or princess. Tailor your desired changes to fit the syndromes which you see are active in your own life.

There are some traps to avoid as you are trying to make life changes. Watch yourself to keep from falling into these traps:

(1) Trying too hard—you try, but you never succeed. You have not given yourself real permission to succeed in changing or

in making friends. There is a time to put forth effort, and there is a time to relax. Realize that it is possible for you to succeed.

(2) Having to do everything just right. This is part of the just-perfect syndrome. This attitude keeps you from celebrating the battles you win because you have not yet won the war. Read again the antidote to just perfect.

(3) Having to do it now. This is the inner drive to make changes overnight. Remember that it took you many years to become the way you are. You can take an appropriate amount of time to make life changes.

(4) Being emotionally strong, refusing to admit the weakness, fears, and need to depend which are in all of us. Admitting your feelings is one important step in changing them.

(5) Pleasing everybody, which is an impossible task! If you are trying to please everyone around you, you are always adapting to someone else. You never get a chance to be yourself. And people do not know how to respond to you. If you do not present a stable picture of yourself but try to mirror what you see in others, they are confused.

If all these changes seem beyond you, remember that the greatest resource you have is your own personality. Within yourself, God has placed all the resources you will need for living a healthy, balanced, growing life. Recall what was said in chapter 3 about God's Spirit being in us. We have all the resources of the universe at our disposal. But the Spirit does not work in a vacuum. He works in and through all the parts of our personalities. So, the more we use all that we are in making life changes, the stronger will be his influence in our lives.

To visualize all these parts of your personality, think of yourself as a giant star. In the center of the star is the *I*—the unique person created by God. Here is where God's Spirit lives and works. Around the *I* are the five points of the star.

The top point, or arm, is your thinking. God has blessed all of us with intelligence. It is there to be used. Are you hearing a little voice saying, "I can't think well"? If so, that is false! You may think differently from your brothers and sisters or some people you went to school with. But you have the ability to reason, to learn, and to process data. Most of us have far more brain power than we ever use in a lifetime. Scientists estimate that even an Einstein uses slightly more than 10 percent of his available brain power.

The two side arms of the star are your judgment and values. Another word for judgment might be *wisdom,* or *common sense.* This arm gives you both protection and permission. It helps you to know when you are getting into danger. It also encourages you to venture into new areas of life. It tells you that it is all right to take some chances and dangerous to take others. The other arm is your value system. It rates your ideas and actions. It tells you what you value most. It sounds an alarm if you are straying away from your values. Your conscience is part of your value system.

The lower arms of the star are your emotions and responses, both natural and learned. The natural emotions are joy, love, sexual feelings, anger, fear, and sadness—or mixtures of these. The emotions are the wellsprings of action. Creativity grows out of love, joy, and the sex drive used as energy to put your gifts to use. Anger and fear trigger actions of self-protection and of aggression against evil. Sadness expresses the sense of loss of something or someone of value. It is closely allied to your value system. Of course, these emotions can be put to wrong uses, just as an automobile can be used to kill as well as to transport people. But when put at the disposal of God's Spirit, in line with your thinking and your judgment, the emotions are of vital importance.

The learned emotions and responses can be both helpful and hindering. A learned fear reaction will cause a person to leap back to the curb when he hears a car approaching. This is a healthy learned response. Another fear reaction may cause people to refuse to go to a high place or to fly in an airplane. This is not a healthy response because it does not fit with reality. Learned emotions may cause a person to block one emotion in favor of another. One who was taught that it was wrong to cry may get angry instead or may laugh at inappropriate moments. Learned responses are more important when people live together in society. No one can always express emotions without consideration for others. But emotions need to be constantly reevaluated to be sure they are appropriate to a person's changing circumstances.

Put your "star" at the disposal of the Spirit of God. This is what self-denial means: You will deny the unhealthy, fearful, child-programmed parts of you so that the healthy, creative self may have full scope to live. This is the aim of God's Spirit in your life.

When you are following who you are, under the guidance of God, you are being your best self. In our competitive society, we are always asking, Who is the best? How can I be the best? These questions are comparative ones, setting one human being against another.

The right answer to these questions, as God would give it, is the answer of the dulcimer maker. Dulcimers are handmade musical instruments. The particular wood used and the shape of the sound hole determine the tone quality of each instrument. When anyone asks the dulcimer maker, "Which is the best one?" his answer is: "There is no best one. They all have different sounds."

This is God's answer about persons. Each one has his or her unique "sound," the expression of the uniqueness created by God.

There are many ways that you can put your "star qualities" to work in making changes in your life. You will need to give yourself much permission to change. Saying, "I can go to a group meeting," or "I can start a conversation with a neighbor" is much stronger than "I ought to go to a group meeting," or "I need to start a conversation with a neighbor." Say these sentences over. See how different you feel after saying them. The first set of sentences builds confidence. The second set leaves you feeling weak and guilty.

Use your thinking ability to realize how ridiculous your old, learned feelings are. If you are afraid to speak to a new person, tell yourself, "I'm scared to speak to new people. . . . I'm scared to speak to the grocery clerk. . . . I'm scared to ask directions at a new service station. . . . I'm scared to talk to a repairman I haven't seen before." As you continue to say these things, your mind will tell you that you are really not scared to talk with strangers. You do it all the time. Then your sense of humor can come to your rescue. As you laugh at the absurdity (not at yourself), you can begin to change the old fear. Talking to strangers whom you wish to have as friends takes skill—the same sort of skill you learned to use in talking with people on a business basis.

Also, watch yourself when you are slipping into old habits. Draw back from yourself to see what you are doing. Use your thinking to see whether this behavior is useful or whether it would be helpful to act in another way. Consult your value system to discover whether the old habit really fits what you believe about friendship and personal expression. Then give yourself internal permission to change the old habit. As you do so, give free rein to your joy in being and your love for other people. In these ways you will be using all that you are to make life changes.

The Depressed Lonely Person

Some persons have a more desperate sense of loneliness than others. They may feel a sense of shame over being lonely. Such an attitude will cut them off from facing their true feelings of loneliness. It will also keep them from associating with persons who are as lonely as they are.

Such persons, on the other hand, may have a real sense of panic over their lonely state. These people rush to find companionship, no matter where or on what basis. Some marriages are built on panic rather than love. Two lonely people think that by marrying they will escape both the pain and stigma of loneliness. But the result is greater loneliness for both, individually and as a couple.

Those who withdraw because of their feelings of loneliness become even more dependent on companionship when they do find it. Few people can live totally alone. So when lonely people turn to others, they are pathetically dependent on the good will and companionship of these others. They are often not able to assert their own independence or to protect themselves against unreasonable demands from their friends.

Persons who are afflicted with a great deal of loneliness adopt many unhealthy ways of coping with their situation. They may overeat to the point of obesity. (This is also a defense against loneliness. If I am so fat, then obviously no one wants to be around me. So no change in my personality would help.) They may drink to the point of becoming alcoholics. They may engage in drug abuse to reduce the pain of loneliness. They may develop disabling diseases or be accident prone. Such difficulties might arouse pity and gain some attention. Sleeplessness, fatigue, and psychosomatic illnesses such as ulcers and headaches can often be traced to loneliness.

By far the greatest problem for lonely people, however, is depression, with its accompanying passivity. Depression is the feeling of almost despair which comes with prolonged loneliness. The person develops the conviction that nothing will ever change; that there is no way out of loneliness.

This is a very passive state. In it the person has little emotional or physical energy. The person shows symptoms of laziness: the inability to get started or to carry out a program; a lot of daydreaming and excessive sleep; refusal to respond to urging from others to do something. But this condition is not true laziness. Beating oneself over the head and calling oneself lazy, good-for-nothing is no help. What the inner person needs is assurance and confidence.

The way to overcome the depression of loneliness is to build up self-esteem. This is done by reprogramming (see the section on changing old tapes about the self) and by getting into personal contact with other persons. At first this will seem almost impossible. But it is like taking vitamins: even a small dose per day begins to build strength. If you are in depression, make it a point each day to get some contacts. They may be with grocery clerks or service station attendants. You probably will not be able at this point to initiate contacts with persons whom you would like to have as friends. Also, have contact with family or with friends every day. Feed on these contacts. Allow them to build up your strength. When you are feeling more energy, get into your program of changing old habits.

6

Learn to Make and Keep Friends

"Everybody needs somebody." But not just any somebody will do. Each person needs friends who help to meet the person's needs and who need what this person has to offer.

In general there are four elements which friends can supply. We need people who *share our concern*. We want people who are concerned about the same things we are, whether it is government, the rearing of children, financial stability, or a good neighborhood. We also need persons *we can depend on in a pinch*. In a community where there is no extended family, we all need people to whom we can turn in an emergency. We need *one or more really close friends*. These are people to whom we can confide some of our inmost thoughts and our deepest feelings. And we need people who will *respect our competence*. We want people who believe in our ability to do things.

Not all of these qualities need to be embodied in one friend. In fact, we may need numbers of friends who can fill one or more of these needs. We may know people who share our concern but are not close friends. We may have friends and neighbors who would be dependable in an emergency but who do not know us well enough to respect our competence.

Making friends, then, is not a matter of finding just two or three people who will be everything we want and need. Just as we need meaningful personal contacts with many people in order to get our needs met healthily, so we need many friends on different levels.

Often this approach is foreign to the lonely person. The

lonely person imagines that getting just one close friend will be the answer to every problem. If he finds a friend, that person bears the weight of the lonely person's needs. No wonder that often such friendships are shortlived! Few persons are able to be all in all to someone. And they certainly will not take such a responsibility on a short acquaintance. Instead, they shrink back and begin to put distance between themselves and a person who seems ready to devour them emotionally.

The thrust of this chapter, then, is on how to make friends, where to find friends, how to keep these friends, and how to deepen relationships so that close friendships are formed.

How to Make Friends

Janet was a lonely person. Finally she got enough courage to try to get out and meet friends. She went to a lecture series, got there late, and sat in the back. All during the lecture she was looking over the other women who were there. Many of them seemed much older than she. Some, she felt, were either too well-off to notice her or too poorly dressed for her to be interested in them. By the time the lecture had ended, she was ready to take flight. A social time was announced, and the audience was invited to stay. But Janet slipped out the back door. Later she told her mother, "There wasn't a single person there that I could imagine being my friend. And not one spoke to me!"

Eleanor was in a similar situation as Janet. She, too, decided to try to make friends. She had learned some techniques, perhaps from reading a book like this one! She was determined to put them into action.

She, too, went to a lecture series. Instead of sitting in the back, she sat toward the front. She spoke to the woman next to her and tried to engage her in conversation. She did not observe that the woman was with someone else and that she was uncomfortable with Eleanor's persistent overtures. Eleanor even leaned over several times during the lecture to whisper comments.

When the woman moved away with her friend after the lecture, Eleanor was offended. She said to herself that the woman was very rude.

Eleanor then went into the social hour. She saw a group of women talking animatedly together, and she joined them. She did not wait to be introduced or to find out what the topic of conversation was. She stood by, impatiently waiting for a chance to interject comments about the lecture, the crowd, and the quality of the food. Much of what she said was critical, and the other women gradually stopped talking. The group broke up, and Eleanor was left alone. She went home thinking, "This advice about making friends is all wet. I did everything they said, and it didn't work."

Janet and Eleanor typify two types of problems which lonely people have in trying to make friends.

Janet, although she was going through the motions of trying to relate to people, was really discounting her ability to solve her problems. She went to a meeting, but she did what she always did: sat in the back, did not speak to people, and left early. By her actions, she was saying that nothing would change her lonely situation. Also, she was discounting the people at the lecture. Instead of looking for possible friends, she was classifying everyone as impossible candidates for friendship. In discounting others, she was also discounting herself. When you can't imagine finding a friend at a group, you are saying that there is no way for another person to relate to you!

Eleanor went a step further than Janet. She at least tried to put some friendship techniques into practice. So she was not discounting her ability to solve the problem of loneliness. But she was wrong in her attitude. She discounted others by not looking at them as persons. They were only things to be manipulated in the hope of making some friends. She did not notice the way she was intruding on the interests and activities of the other people. And she discounted herself by not allowing herself to relax and enjoy the lecture and social time. Whether she made a new friend or not, she could have enjoyed being with herself!

Attitudes toward other persons and toward oneself are always more important than techniques. In the popular phrase, the lonely person must seek to relate to others on an "I'm OK—you're OK" basis. This phrase means that I am a person of worth and I respect you as a person of worth. I allow you the privilege of relating to me or not relating to me. If you do not relate to me, I'm still OK. If you begin to relate to me, and I find that we don't blend, I allow myself the privilege of not continuing the acquaintance. And I can do that while still thinking you are a person of worth.

Too often persons seek to relate in two other ways: either "I'm not OK—you're OK" or "I'm OK—you're not OK." The first stance is the one that many lonely people have. They have failed in friendships so many times that they think everyone is better than they are. They truly do not think of themselves as worthy to have friends. If this is your stance, you need to review self-esteem in chapter 5 and work hard on those exercises.

The second stance also involves some lonely people. They do not have friends because they are constantly putting other people down. Friendship is a give-and-take relationship. The person who thinks, "I'm OK—you're not OK," is not willing to have such a relationship. She is always wanting people who will constantly give in to her demands. If you have this attitude, you need to deal with yourself according to the prince or princess syndrome in chapter 5.

Such attitudes do not change overnight. Nor is it necessary to wait to make friends until the attitude is just right. In fact, the very effort of making friends tends to change a person's attitudes. As he opens to the possibility of friendships, there is more sense of self-esteem and more willingness to share with others.

Now for some practical suggestions about making friends. *First, get involved in groups where you have a legitimate interest and where you can expect to meet the kinds of persons you want to have as friends.* If you are involved in groups where you have an interest, you can have a good time whether you make friends or not. Also, you will be more comfortable in such a group. It is important to feel that you belong when you get into a group.

If you want to meet certain types of people, the quickest way is to find groups that will include a good percentage of such persons. This is the reason why lonely hearts clubs, some singles groups, and "herds" that include all kinds of people are not good starting places for friendship. Such groups are based on the lowest common denominator principle. Everyone is single, lonely, out looking, as in some bars. But when you have said that, you have said everything you know about the group. A lonely person, looking for someone with an interest in art, football, or conversational Spanish is going to have a hard time sifting through all the persons in a herd to find his special interest.

So, the first thing to do is to inventory your interests and abilities. What do you like to do—sports, hobbies, educational pursuits, or service? What are you interested in knowing more about or getting more involved in? Make a list of all these interests, no matter how vague. Perhaps some of these interests were ones you had years ago but have dropped. Add them. Then look for clubs, organizations, and church groups which emphasize some of your interests.

If you go where your interest lies, you will automatically have something in common with the other persons there. You may even know more about the subject than some of the people. Thus you will be more interesting to them. And you will already have a basis for acquaintance and perhaps friendship through a shared interest.

Second, give yourself permission to feel at home in the group which you are attending. This is a lot harder, but it is very important. If you feel out of place or uncomfortable, other people will feel uncomfortable around you.

When you get ready to attend a meeting, remind yourself that you belong to this group because of your interests. You do not need to sell yourself to the other members. You already belong. Then go with the idea of enjoying being with this group.

I had a unique experience in this area when I attended my high school class reunion a couple of years ago. I had never been to a reunion and had lost touch with all but one of my high school classmates. But this was a special reunion. I still was not planning to go because it was near Louisville, Kentucky, and I live in Texas. But after receiving a call from the class president, I decided to go.

Still, I was afraid. I had been (in my mind) the class ugly duckling. I was afraid I would be ignored by the others. But a friend of mine wisely gave me a challenge: "Go to the reunion without trying to sell yourself. For the first hour, just greet people and respond to their questions."

I accepted the challenge with reservations. But to my delighted surprise, it worked! Everyone spoke to me, asked me about myself, told me about themselves. I didn't have to do a thing! Later one of the men wrote me that several had agreed I was "the best-looking one" at the reunion. So much for the ugly duckling!

Knowing that you belong will give you an assurance. This attitude will help you to fit into groups and begin to make friends.

A technique to use in order to feel at home is to find a "secure place" in the group. A single man whom I know has an effective way of feeling at home in a new group. He pauses when entering a room and surveys the surroundings. Then he decides which part of the room will be his "home." It may be a comfortable chair, a seat in a corner, or a place near the refreshment table. Wherever it is, he heads straight for that place and claims it for his own. He stays in or near that place until he feels comfortable enough with the crowd to move out. If he begins to feel uncomfortable at a later time, he moves "back home" until he regains his assurance.

This simple technique can become a trap if you stay in your "safe place," never venturing out. But it is a good plan for feeling at home quickly in a strange place.

Third, use various approaches in contacting people and beginning a relationship. In beginning to make friends, don't gravitate toward the most popular. These people are busy with friends and activities. They may be friendly, but they will not be as apt to be looking for new friends.

Instead, look around for persons and couples who are sitting alone. These people, like you, are probably at the meeting hoping to find new acquaintances.

Your approach to these people should be light, not heavy-handed. Remember, if they are feeling lonely, they will be scared off by a strong approach, just as you would be. You can begin a conversation by finding out whether they, like you, are new members. You can express your views of the program or your ideas about what is going on in the organization.

Conversation is the way to friendship. But conversation should not be intrusive. There are certain topics which may be safely treated, leading to more personal matters as trust between persons is established. So people begin by talking about things: the weather or the price of meat at the supermarket. They progress to talking about ideas and people: such ideas as what is being discussed at the group meeting; such persons as the head of the organization, local personalities of interest, and government officials (so long as the talk doesn't get too political). The next level of conversation is the exchange of personal information—the kinds of topics that would be covered in an interview or a biographical sketch: Where did you live before you came here? What kind of work do you do? How much family do you have? The last, and deepest, level of conversation is the one where personal feelings, convictions, hopes, and dreams are shared.

By following this pattern of conversation, you will find that you and your potential friends can build trust and confidence in each other without too much risk. Sometimes, like strangers on a plane, two people begin to share too much too soon. Then they feel uncomfortable: What is this person thinking about what I have just said. The next reaction is to pull away. Strangers on a plane can share because they will never see each other again. Two people who have begun to get acquainted may feel the same impulse to separate when they have shared deeply. So it is much wiser to begin on lower levels of communication. Leave the more personal and intimate interchanges for later stages of friendship.

Making friends can become an exciting adventure if you look for innovative ways of getting acquainted. Remember that everyone feels pretty much as you do: They want to meet people, but they do not always know how to go about it. They often will respond with gratitude to a skillful advance.

I had this experience in a national meeting of psychotherapists. I felt at home in the conference, and I had my own friends with me. But I wanted to meet others. It seemed that people were just talking with those whom they knew. How could I break in?

I thought about it for a good while, and then came up with this plan: The psychotherapists made much of the idea of having contracts about things they, or their clients, were going to do. So I decided to make a contract with myself to meet four new people in the space of half an hour.

I walked up to a person and said, "I've made a contract to meet four new people before 1:30. Will you be one of them?" Of course, no one refused! In fact, I met about six in half an hour.

I didn't make any lasting friends by using this technique.

But it broke the ice for me in speaking to new people. Also, some of the persons I met kept turning up in workshops during the conference. It was nice to find familiar faces—faces that I had made contact with.

Other ways to meet new people are to ask for help from another member of the group and to offer your help to the group. Everyone enjoys being able to give help; so a member will probably feel good about helping you. Telling you something about the organization, pointing out the officers, or showing the way to the rest room are all ways that others can help you.

When you offer help, be sure to offer it to the group, not to an individual, unless that person has asked for it. Giving unsolicited help can be an "I'm OK—you're not OK" ploy. In effect you are saying that you know better than the other person what her needs are and that you are better able to supply those needs.

This rescuing attitude is a trap into which lonely people easily fall. They often feel a lack of identity. Feeling that someone is dependent on them gives them status, even if only for a few minutes. This sense of status can keep the lonely person from seeking his own identity in the group. So long as someone is dependent on him, there is a sense of security.

But this is a highly manipulative attitude. Some people want to be dependent on others; they are basically "I'm not OK—you're OK" people. When a dependent person meets a helping one, an unhealthy relationship can be set up. The dependent person constantly finds new ways for the helper to be of use. And the helper presses the dependent person to be increasingly dependent. Some friendships develop in this way. But they are basically unstable. They are not based on give-and-take on both sides. One side is all give and the other is all take. Eventually this unhealthy balance breaks down. The result is hurt feelings and greater loneliness on both sides.

Offering help to the group is a much healthier approach. Taking notes at a meeting, serving on a committee, working on a project, or simply running an errand can signal your interest in the group. Healthy group members put the concerns of the group above their own. Helpful actions on your part show your concern, and they also bond your sense of belonging to the group. Other members will notice your interest and therefore notice you.

I have known people who could not feel at home in a gathering unless they were doing something. For such persons, the actions of helpfulness give them a sense of belonging which they cannot achieve within themselves. If this is your problem, by all means be helpful. But also recognize your feeling of isolation which will not allow you to relax in a group. Work on your self-esteem until you can feel at home with a group simply because you are there.

As you begin to make friends—in a Sunday School class, in a PTA group, in a bowling league—allow these persons to relate to you according to their desires and according to your own. Pressing a relationship too far too soon can cause it to go sour. And if you feel pressed by the other person, your fears will cause you to pull away.

It is important to have many friends, on many levels of closeness. Your impulse may be to hunt for that one "perfect" friend who will meet all your needs. Instead, follow the example of Jesus. He did not have one special friend. He was not married. He refused to be bound by family ties. He had an inner circle of three special friends among his twelve immediate followers. But he did not look to them to meet all his needs. There were others to whom he related warmly: Mary and Martha, Mary Magdalene, Nicodemus, and Joseph of Arimathea.

The principle Jesus seemed to follow was to have many friends on various levels: casual acquaintances, friends whom he saw only infrequently, close associates, and intimate friends. His example gives us a pattern of healthy relationships.

So begin by building multilevel relationships. These will include casual acquaintances, people whom you meet at work, at church, in the neighborhood, or at social affairs. You may have little sustained contact with them. But you see them regularly, and you can get some support from them on a light basis.

Other friends might be those whom I call one-theme friends. These are people with whom you share a mutual interest. I have had friends with whom I did nothing except bowl, go bird-watching, or attend a symphony concert. But these mutual interests can build up pleasant friendships with a minimum of emotional risk.

Of course, some of the people you meet will be attracted to you as a friend, and you to them. You may find some of your already existing relationships beginning to deepen. You may reach out to others to see whether they are willing to have a closer relationship. If not, you need not be devastated. The support of your network of friends can keep you from feeling emotionally bereft. You will not be putting all your eggs in one or two baskets.

Don't overlook the possibility of some of your "lower-level" friendships growing into deeper intimacy. I had a friend with whom I did nothing except plant a garden every year. But time went by and circumstances changed. She became one of my best friends.

As you look for friends, continue to cultivate the attitude that make friendships possible. Be willing to trust people. This does not mean a blind trust that takes everyone at face value and often is hurt. It means a willingness to risk a relationship with the knowledge that you may sometimes be disappointed. It means, also, that you will be willing to let people trust you.

Approach making friends with an attitude of hope. Look

forward to finding new relationships. This attitude of expectancy will be evident to other people, and they will move toward you.

How to Deal with Situational Loneliness

Some loneliness is especially painful because it is connected with being in a new place or a new situation in life. A person or a couple who move to a new locality have particular problems in making friends. And those who have become single again, through death or divorce, are usually thrust into devastating loneliness.

The problems of the single-again group are compounded by the fact that they have friends all around them. But these friends no longer relate to them in the same way. The single person is out of place in a couples' society. Both the single person and the married friends feel this acutely. At first it really is better for the divorced or widowed person to seek the companionship of others who are in the same situation. When one has been grievously wounded, it is hard to relate to persons who are still whole.

Fortunately there are more and more organizations and groups that deal with widowed and/or divorced persons. The ones who are newly singled can find many of their needs met through these groups. After they have made their adjustments to their changed situation, both divorced and widowed persons are better able to relate to people on the basis of interest and attraction, whether these people are married or single.

One word of caution: Groups that work with the newly singled should be carefully checked out before getting involved in them. Church singles groups and other service-type organizations for single persons can offer special help to the newly divorced and widowed. These would be my personal preference in lieu of dating services and singles groups that charge fees for getting people together.

For persons moving to a new locality, the general problems of making friends are compounded by the sense of strangeness in a different place. Learning the routes to work, school, grocery, and shopping centers takes time and energy. Often the climate and the customs are very different, increasing the sense of strangeness. So it is necessary to take the step to friendship in two stages.

First, become familiar with your territory. Locate the supermarket, drugstore, bank, and service station which you will be using. On your first trip to each place, introduce yourself and explain that you are a newcomer. Don't expect the service personnel to guess this simply because your face is unfamiliar. These persons see many strange faces daily. Let them know that you are interested in their services. Learn their names, and thank them for services rendered. Within a few weeks, you will feel that you do have some friends as you continue to go to these places. If you work downtown, follow the same technique at the bank, at the restaurant where you will eat most often, and at the department store where you may do most of your shopping.

Read your newspaper carefully to find notices and information about various organizations and clubs in which you may be interested. Join one or two of these as soon as possible. They will give you the chance to make friends quickly.

Get in touch with a dentist and a physician. Ask to be put on the patient list of each one. If the physician wants you to have a general physical, get one. It is important to be in contact with a health professional in case of an emergency. Such assurance will make you feel part of the community.

Most important, promptly transfer your membership to a church. You should not do this, however, before "shopping around" for a while. Look for a church which embodies several of the qualities suggested in chapter 4. Also, find a church whose worship services and educational approaches fit what you are used to. But, as soon as you have found such a church, join it. Get involved in as many activities as you have time and inclination for. Soon you will be feeling at home in your church home.

Also, if you hold membership in a lodge or a service organization, transfer your membership to a local body. Again, the more people to whom you can relate quickly, the sooner you will feel at home in your new community.

Persons living in the suburbs or in apartments may have some real difficulty in crashing the neighborhood. Suburbanites tend to live within their own properties. And it is common for apartment dwellers not to know the names of their next-door neighbors.

Being friendly to neighbors without acting intrusive is the best approach. Tell the neighbor your name (and your spouse's). Express your pleasure at being in this neighborhood. Respond to any friendly approach that the neighbor makes. By continuing to be open, you pave the way for a better acquaintance. But if your neighbors choose not to be friendly, don't take this personally. Some people are afraid to make friends in the area for fear that their privacy will be invaded. They do not know how to set limits on their friends. So they simply close the door to neighborliness.

However, more and more neighbors are banding together for mutual protection. Persons in the same area watch out for each other's property when the neighbors are out of town or at work. They stand ready to help each other when needed. But they do not run in and out of each other's houses or expect to be included in each other's social affairs.

Where to Find Friends

Where do you find groups that share your interests? Unless you live in a very small town, there is no lack of choices. Look at the following categories. Mark the ones which strike your interest. Then check your telephone directory yellow pages (under clubs, societies, and social service organizations) to find local groups. You may also call your Chamber of Commerce, United Way, library information, and other sources to find names and telephone numbers for groups in which you are interested.

Economic groups: service clubs, chamber of commerce, labor unions, professional organizations

Governmental groups: political party organizations, good government leagues, League of Women Voters, veterans associations

Educational groups: PTA, adult education classes or societies, college alumni societies

Fraternal groups: fraternities and sororities or lodges

Recreational groups: athletic teams or clubs, booster clubs, hobby clubs, social clubs

Religious groups: churches and synagogues and their groupings (see chapter 4)

Cultural groups: concert societies, art or drama societies, little theater, cultural study groups, book clubs

Welfare groups: charitable associations, welfare or humane associations (do volunteer work with these groups)

Groups for children or youth: child welfare or youth organizations, Big Brother or Big Sister

Health groups: community health, groups related to specific diseases—cancer, heart, arthritis, birth defects, etc.

Nature and conservation groups: Audubon Society; Sierra Club; local nature, park, and wildlife conservation groups

For newcomers to a community, there are opportunities to know the neighbors through various means. Newcomers may join a bowling league and ask to be put on a team with longtime residents of the community. A newcomer may sponsor a Tupperware party and invite the whole neighborhood. Block parties, which are increasingly popular, are wonderful ways to meet the people on the street. Being a volunteer for the American Heart Association or the March of Dimes opens doors all up and down the street. A newcomer can meet neighbors within the space of an hour or so. And in many areas there are Newcomers Clubs which give new residents a chance to know one another.

It is important to get involved both in groups of like-minded people and with one's neighbors. The interest groups provide stimulation and chances for real friendship. But there is no substitute for good neighbors. These are the people who will pick up the papers when you are out of town, look after your pets and house plants, and keep an eye on your property. In an emergency, they are the nearest source of help.

In choosing your interest groups, be careful not to get involved in too many at once. There is danger in spreading yourself too thin. The object is not to belong to a lot of groups but to become active in a few. In-depth involvement will bring you more opportunities for friendship than being a superficial member.

How to Keep Friends

People often wonder why it is easier for them to make friends than to keep them. Two people initially get very interested in each other. But as they continue to see each other, the interest wanes. Boredom, suspicion, or even dislike may take its place. Finally, either one or both decide that the friendship was a mistake, and they part.

How can one avoid this sad ending to what seemed to be the start of a good friendship? Of course, this is bound to happen sometimes. But there are special qualities that turn a passing acquaintance into a good friendship. All of us have these qualities; we need to cultivate them.

Use all that you are in developing a friendship.—Review what is said in chapter 5 about all the facets of your personality:

thinking, judgment, value system, natural emotions, and learned emotions and responses. Often a person will use only a limited portion of these facets in making friends. Without expanding the sharing of self with a friend, there is little basis for a well-rounded friendship.

I had this kind of experience with a man a few years ago. We met at a party where everyone was very light and gay. We enjoyed laughing together and playing jokes on the other people. The next day he called and asked to meet me for lunch the following week. I told him that I would have a busy day, but I could take a couple of hours out for lunch.

When we met, I was no longer in the fun-loving mood. I tried to talk with him about his interests and mine. But he insisted on making everything a joke. When I did not respond, the gleam of interest in his eye rapidly faded. We got back before my two hours was up—and I never heard from him again. The basis of our acquaintance had been totally on one level. It was not enough to build on for friendship.

So, as you relate to persons, take care that they see all the facets of your personality: the serious things you are interested in; the way you care about others, particularly these persons; the values you find important, both negative and positive; your feelings, whether these be joy, love, creativity, anger, fear, or sadness; and some of your hang-ups that cause you to react as you do. These should not all be unloaded at one time. But if you are honestly sharing yourself with another person, you will find ways to bring these facets into the open.

Being seen as a many-faceted person will make you much more interesting to your friends. Dr. Stephen Karpman, a California psychiatrist who emphasizes this approach, tells an amusing story about one of his clients. She was good at getting first dates. But after two or, at the most, three dates the men tended to disappear. She had been using her fun-loving side to get dates, but she never revealed anything further. Dr. Karpman explained to her the importance of letting the men see more than one side of her. He challenged her to use all that she had. At the next session, she reported that her current date had been impressed with her and wanted a date the next night.

Dr. Karpman asked her what she had done. Her eyes dancing, she reported: "I wanted to be sure that I would get all the facets in. So I timed myself. Every fifteen minutes I would change the emphasis, no matter where we were in the conversation. He seemed confused a couple of times, but he sure wasn't bored!"

It is not necessary to take such a literal approach to sharing. But as you open up the facets of your personality, you also make it possible for your friend to share more honestly with you. And this sharing is the true basis of friendship.

Use options to avoid unhealthy reactions in conflict. — Conflict is inevitable in any friendship that goes beyond the superficial. There will be disagreements, disapproval, and misunderstandings from time to time. Using "all that you are" can help you to avoid serious conflict when these times of tension come.

Most of us, in a time of tension, respond according to learned responses. If a person flies off the handle easily, he will almost automatically use that response in conflict. Another person may cry, withdraw, or try to make a joke out of the situation.

It is important to know that we have many more ways of responding than the ones we learned in childhood. Jesus explained options in the Sermon on the Mount. Most people, when they were treated unfairly, tended to react in kind. But Jesus reminded his hearers that they had other ways of acting: If they had to carry a Roman soldier's pack for a mile, they could opt for carrying it another mile. If they were slapped on one cheek, they had the option of offering the other rather than striking back. Jesus made it clear that human beings can act according to their own choices, not in blind reaction.

Suppose you and your new friend have a conflict over punctuality. Your friend is chronically late, at least fifteen minutes. You, on the other hand, like to get places as early as you can. How can you resolve this conflict without losing a friendship which you otherwise enjoy?

Consider how you can use the various facets of personality—both yours and your friend's—to come to agreement. You can both *think* of ways that take care of your needs: You can decide to meet at a halfway point, where you plan to arrive ten minutes after your friend is scheduled to arrive. Or you set the time of departure fifteen minutes early, so that your friend can be late and still be on time. You will need to decide how early is early enough and make concessions about that.

You can *care* enough for each other to accommodate to each other's internal time clock. Some people simply get things done faster than others.

You can decide how much *value* you put on being on time. Sometimes it is more important to be on time, as at a concert or a play. Other times it is better to be a little late, as when you are arriving at the home of a friend for dinner.

You can honestly share with your friend your *feelings* about not being on time. These probably will include anger and perhaps fear. You need not fly off the handle to show your anger. You can say, "I really get angry when we are late because I'm scared that people will look at us and think we are rude for not being on time." Many of us are not trained to express feelings openly. This is the reason why we often wait until we are so full of feelings that we explode. If you are not accustomed to expressing your feelings, practice what you are going to say. Be sure that this is really the way you feel. Most people can learn to accept honest feelings if they are not threatened by the violence of the other person's emotions.

You can also tell your friend why you have such a compulsion—a *learned response*—to get places early. Such a confession can open the way for the friend to state why he or she feels such a need to be late.

Using one or more of these options can be a constructive response in a conflict situation. An option can point the way to a better solution. It also can deepen friendship as two people share their feelings about a matter on which they differ.

Be honest with your feelings; don't harbor grudges. —This is an expansion on what has been said about options. True friendship is never built on pretense. People who pretend not to be hurt, angry, or scared when they really are will undermine the friendship. Unexpressed feelings don't disappear; they go underground. Like a splinter in a finger, they fester. Later they make their presence known through outbursts of emotion that often are out of proportion to the immediate cause.

Learn to express your feelings in words, not in actions or body language. Be honest with these feelings and try to give a rationale for the way you feel. Such openness makes friendship a more truly two-way street. One friend feeling free to express feelings, gives the other friend the same freedom.

Avoid being a rescuer or a victim in your friendships.— Recall what was said about persons who like to have people dependent on them and about those who want to depend all the time. A person who sets out to be an eternal helper soon finds that he is stuck in that role. No matter how much he needs to depend, the role is set. Often the result is that the "helpful" friend then becomes "hurtful." He is angry because of unmet dependency needs. So he may lash out at the friend who is being helped, in most unexpected and undesirable ways.

On the other hand, the person who presents herself as a

victim, always needing to be helped, can get stuck in that role. The person may enjoy always being the center of someone else's attention and concern. But the victim may also get to the place where she "would rather do it myself." Then the person finds that the helper is not always willing to give up that role. One result may be that the victim, trying to get out of the dependency, may turn on the helper.

Whatever the role being played, the end result is usually a loss of friendship. Mutual dependence should be the rule in friendship. A friend who always wants to treat at meals, or who is always wanting to be picked up, is not acting healthily. We all have our times of weakness and of strength. We need to act out of these as it is appropriate and necessary. In this way each person has respect for the other's strong points and concern for the other's weak points.

Be concerned for the quality of the relationship: work out of love.—This love is basically a reverence for the other person—which is involved in the respect and concern mentioned earlier. Each person is a separate, unique individual. This is one reason why we seek friendships with other people: They are different from us. They supplement us by their differences. Love means to allow the other person to be *other* and to rejoice in the difference.

Cherish your friendships, even the ones that you know will disappear.—One reason some people avoid friendships is that they wish to avoid the pain of loss. But every relationship carries with it the risk of loss, for whatever reason. The marriage ceremony rightly states the possibility of death as the separation point for the couple.

In our fluid society, people are forever moving away, getting married, becoming single again, changing jobs, and finding new interests. It is impossible to hold on to friendships forever. This knowledge should make our friends even more precious to us. We should cherish them while they are available to us. And when they are gone, we should, with hope, look around for new friends to fill the gaps they have left. We do not replace persons as friends, but we can replenish their gifts to us through finding new friends.

How to Deepen Friendships

Human beings need two kinds of friendships. They need breadth of relationship—friends who span different interests and who offer variety. They also need depth of relationship—friends with whom they can bare their souls, giving and receiving warmth and understanding. Persons need many friends in the breadth category; but two or three in-depth friends are the most anyone can expect or need. In fact, a person would be emotionally worn out trying to relate in depth to more than a few people.

As has been emphasized in this book, the breadth relationships take the pressure off the close friends in having to meet all the needs of the person. But the close friends provide intimacy which the broader relationships do not have.

Closeness requires understanding.—One of our greatest needs as persons is to be understood. In fact, the opposite of loneliness is understanding. Certain things happen as two persons seek to understand each other.

We give the gift of ourselves. No one can be understood through a mask or a false front. If you want to be understood, you must be open with your friend. And this openness needs to be spontaneous. Guarded, well-thought-out confidences reveal their false basis. Certainly, you will be open to misunderstanding when you let yourself go in revelation to another person. But this is part of the process in deepening friendship.

Such revelation requires both trust and time. We do not reveal ourselves without trusting the other person. But one who trusts too quickly is not wise. Relationships need to be tested to see whether they will bear the stress of self-revelation. The wise person reveals bit by bit, observing how these pieces of self are received by the friend. If the result is condemnation, lack of comprehension, or a flippant attitude, then the person knows that this relationship is not going to get to a deep level.

The one who willingly listens and tries to understand also gives the gift of self. Such a person must lay aside individual biases and preconceived notions in order to listen creatively to a friend's confidences. It is not important for the friends to see everything the same way. It is important for one friend to hear the other as she really is and to accept that person.

Such hearing requires love on the part of the friend. He must be able to accept the friend, warts and all, without prejudice. Acceptance does not mean approval. But willingness to understand even those actions that cause pain shows true love. Remember that God loved us even when we "were dead in trespasses and sins." We cannot match that love, but we can seek to follow it.

Closeness requires dialogue.—Dialogue means much more than conversation. It means a process of sharing ideas, attitudes, and feelings in an ever-deepening stream. Recall the stages of conversation discussed earlier in this chapter: from things to abstract ideas and persons in general to sharing personal information to sharing feelings. Dialogue is concerned with the last stage.

Sharing in dialogue must be reciprocal, spontaneous, at times nonverbal, and at all times loving. Like understanding, dialogue is not something that people can put on like a false front. Because of these characteristics, dialogue involves trust on both sides. Trust means not only that I can trust you with my deepest thoughts but also that I am one who can be trusted. This is a commitment between friends. It may not be stated, but it must be understood.

Dialogue also involves hope. Each time two people share with each other on a deep level, hope is raised that such sharing can continue. It will even grow deeper. Such hope will make room for mistakes and times of misunderstanding. If two people have been trusting each other, they can forgive lapses. They have hope that the dialogue can continue, in spite of a temporary break in understanding.

Most of all, dialogue involves love. It takes self-giving love to share deeply with another and to receive that person's sharing. This will also be a self-denying love. Each person must deny his or her fearful, prejudiced, narrow self in order to affirm another self: the true self of understanding, joy, love, and growth in relationship. Two people who love each other enough to want to share with each other will find themselves blossoming as persons.

Dialogue is the climate in which personal growth can take place. When another person shares my thoughts and understands my nature, I can open myself to new possibilities of life. Stunted growth takes place when a person feels that some of the most intimate feelings and thoughts have to be hidden away. The energy devoted to keeping these parts hidden is diverted from emotional and spiritual growth.

How to Be Married to Your Best Friend

All that has been said about deepening friendships should apply to marriage partners. Two people who are committed to each other for life in love, hope, and trust should be able to share with each other deeply. The tragedy of many marriages is that such sharing does not take place. Or, if it does, the sharing tends to dwindle under the pressures of life. Someone has said that a good way to tell married couples from dating couples in a restaurant is to observe which ones are talking to each other. The married couples do not talk!

Too often persons marry in order to get all their needs filled by their partner. When this does not happen, disillusionment sets in. Persons cease to share with their spouses. Eventually two strangers are living in the same house. Unfortunately these strangers think they really know their spouse. They have learned certain facets of the other's personality. Then they build a whole relationship on this limited knowledge. Many lonely married persons would be astonished to know what amazing vistas lie beyond the limited views they have of the persons who face them across the breakfast table.

If yours is a lonely marriage, what can you do about it? Both partners will have to work at the problem, but it can be solved. The husband and wife need to go back and repeat the stages of keeping friends and deepening friendships until they have come to a deep level of sharing. Some couples may even have to go back to the stage of making friends!

It is unfortunate that this kind of effort at friend-making and friend-keeping is too often lavished on a new man or woman. Hoping for stimulation and understanding, husband or wife seeks out a new potential partner. The husband or wife does not realize that an exciting person is waiting at home to be discovered.

A married couple I know, who are constantly deepening their relationship, have a custom they call kidnapping. On special occasions, such as birthdays and anniversaries, one partner will kidnap the other. The spouse will tell the partner to be ready at a certain time, perhaps dressed in a certain way. Then the spouse takes the mate out for an evening, or even a weekend, of entertainment and recreation. Part of the fun is the suspense and the uncertainty felt by the kidnaped mate. And the kidnaper has the satisfaction of planning a delightful time. In the process, they discover new facets of each other in these unusual situations.

So a husband and wife might engage in a friend-making series of dates. They might arrange to meet at an unusual place, to do something they have not done for years, perhaps. In new settings, persons who seem too familiar may take on new faces.

Couples who are seeking to recover a depth of relationship must beware of old grudges. In some cases there may be so much old garbage being carried around that no real friendship can form. If every disagreement includes grievances going back to the beginning of the marriage, the pair will be hopelessly dead-locked. Who can defend himself or herself against things done ten or twenty years ago? So a renewed friendship may need to include wholesale forgiveness on both sides. Read Psalm 103:8-12 to see the quality and extent of the forgiveness that is needed.

Married partners can also learn to use options in dealing with each other. Doing so will break old patterns. It will also disclose new and delightful aspects of each other's character. Nowhere do we behave out of old habits so much as in our homes. Learning new ways to act can revitalize a marriage!

Having broken some old patterns, the couple can go on to deeper intimacy. The physical intimacies in marriage are designed to supplement emotional and spiritual intimacy. But often sexual intimacy remains the only closeness. Then partners complain of too much sameness in sex. Understanding and dialogue can bring new life into the marriage. These are the elements of intimacy. When two people share deeply, their physical closeness is enhanced by their spiritual closeness. Then they discover that they are truly best friends!

Replenish Your Family with Friends

For most people, there is not enough family. Either their family members are widely scattered or there have been losses by death. Often families are not close to one another for the reasons outlined in earlier chapters.

Everyone, even the loneliest persons, can have unlimited family! Anyone who has a broad spectrum of friends, of various ages and both sexes, can have a large family. Persons of the same age group can be cousins or brothers and sisters. Younger people can provide nieces and nephews or even grandchildren. Older people can be aunts and uncles or perhaps grandparents.

After all, the true test of family feeling is not blood ties but love and acceptance. Friends can provide all the emotional support and companionship that we would like to have from family members. A person can build a whole substitute family from the ranks of friends. But this will mean building an intergenerational network of friends. This is not hard to do if persons relate to each other as friends without putting up age barriers. There is no reason people should not have friends twenty years older or younger than themselves. Nor do there have to be barriers of sex or marital status. Love and friendship can leap barriers as long as there is trust, and hope, and love.

7

Learn to Live
with Your Lonely Times

"Saturday night is the loneliest night in the week." "One is the loneliest number." "All alone by the telephone." These themes have been heard many times in popular music. They express the idea that to be alone is to be automatically lonely. So, whether married or single, persons dread the idea of being alone, even for a few hours.

Of course, urelieved loneliness, such as comes with the loss of a mate or with a move from the family home, can be very unpleasant. One woman reported that she called "Time of Day" in the middle of the night simply to hear a human voice. No matter that this was a recording; for a moment she could imagine being in touch with another person.

A couple of years ago I found these statements: "Loneliness describes the pain of being alone. . . . Solitude expresses the glory of being alone."[1] So the effect of being alone is largely determined by the way one handles the alone times.

For the person who does not like himself, such times can be torture. Often one fears to know the self that lies below the surface of everyday busy life. What sort of demons, fears, or ugliness might be revealed if one had to face the person in the mirror? But the opposite may also be true: Behind the everyday face may be undreamed-of courage, beauty, and creativity. It may take some alone time to unveil that face. If so, then being alone will be solitude, not loneliness. And what is discovered will be glory, not pain.

There are other advantages to solitude. We need a counterbalance to closeness. Too much closeness, even in marriage, can be exhausting. So marriage partners need times of being alone.

Solitary times give opportunities for making decisions and tapping inner resources. Persons who have to live alone find—often to their surprise—that they have many more resources for life than they imagined.

Creativity is brought to fruition in solitude. The artist cannot work in a hubbub. Imagination, new ideas, and creative energy spring to life during the alone times. This is the reason very few creative ideas are born in a committee! I found this to be true when I was working on a committee planning some Bible curriculum. I would try to think, but my mind refused to work. Finally, I would leave the room and pace up and down the hall for ten or fifteen minutes. Both the activity and the solitude released my thought processes. I realized that being with other people who were discussing their thoughts tended to inhibit my own creativity.

Our urban society makes times of solitude necessary. Many persons in the mental health field believe that solitude is necessary for emotional well-being. They say that an inability to engage in solitary reflection is one of the major causes of emotional illness in our culture. We are all deluged with noise, surrounded by people, assaulted by smells and pollution, overstimulated by things to see. These are called "ego impingements." They bombard our selves so that we begin to lose the sense of who we are. Solitude can bring relief from these impingements. But it must be a solitude that is natural, avoiding the use of radio and TV, which create an illusion of not being alone.

Most of all, solitude provides the opportunity for deepening one's relationship with God. Fellowship times with other Christians are important. But, as in every deep friendship, there must be the opportunity for intimate, one-to-one sharing. Every great

Christian has testified to the importance of quiet times. There must be solitude in which to speak to God and to listen to God's voice.

Let us consider these aspects of solitude and how any person can use them to grow spiritually and emotionally.

Discover Yourself in Solitude

Most of us do not know ourselves very well. Often we have concentrated on the less admirable parts, totally ignoring our best selves. I had a counseling client once who did that in a dramatic way. Her picture of herself when she was depressed was of a slovenly woman, with dirty, unkept hair, without animation. When she was depressed, she came to the counseling group dressed the way she looked to herself: Her hair was unwashed and pulled back under a scarf. She wore faded jeans, a work shirt, and scuffed moccasins. Her face was devoid of makeup—and of expression.

As she continued to come to the counseling group, she learned more about herself. She discovered a happy, playful, intelligent person. When she was feeling good, she came looking like that person. Her hair would be newly washed and set. She would wear becoming clothes and tasteful makeup. She looked and acted like a different person. But every time the old depression surfaced, everyone in the counseling group knew it immediately. She would revert to her "awful" self, as she termed it. It was very difficult to convince her that the true self was more the happy person than the bedraggled one.

There are certain techniques that you can follow in discovering yourself. Begin with being in tune with your body. The biblical view of personality is that we are all "of a piece"—body, mind, emotions, and spirit. We cannot neglect or ignore one part without damaging the whole. But most people tend to think of the body as an adjunct to personality, not an integral part of it. They ignore signals of both discomfort and pleasure from their bodies. They go on as if they could do anything, in spite of what their bodies might be telling them.

I read an important statement from a physician: "The body has a wisdom all its own, and we all would do well to heed it." The body can tell us when to eat, when to sleep, when to get exercises, when to provide stimulation through being with others. But we have so long tuned out the signals from the body that it may take some time to be sensitive to these signals again. We had these signals in abundance in childhood. But we have schooled ourselves to pay them no attention. We have learned to eat and to go to bed at certain times. No matter whether we are hungry or sleepy at those times.

So the first step is to get in better touch with your body. This can be done by a simple relaxation exercise. Sit comfortably in a chair or lie flat on a bed. Beginning with your head, quietly allow yourself to relax. Smooth out your forehead, close your eyes, relax cheeks, mouth, and chin. Relax your neck muscles and then your shoulders. Let go the tension in your arms, beginning with your shoulders and extending to your fingertips. As you relax your fingers, allow the tension to slip out of them and into the air. Then relax your chest, your diaphragm, your stomach, and your abdomen. Use the same relaxing technique with your legs that you used with your arms, allowing the tension to flow out of your toes.

After doing this exercise, remain quiet for several minutes, paying close attention to your body. Where does the tension first tend to come back? Where is the relaxation most pronounced and most pleasurable? Where in your body do you feel best? Where do you feel worst?

As you continue to do this exercise daily, you will learn a lot. First, you will learn better how to relax. You may find this extremely difficult at first. But with practice you will relax more quickly. You will also learn which parts of your body hoard tension. These are the last to relax and the first to tense up. They probably also are the first places where you may feel illness. A tense stomach is apt to get upset easily. A tense back can easily produce pain.

Second, you will learn to commune with your body. You will be more aware of it and of the signals it sends out. You will know better when you are tired, need to eliminate, are thirsty, or need food. You will feel a need for exercise or for relaxation, as your muscles tense up. As you know more about your body's communication system, you probably will find yourself in better rhythm with your body's needs. Many people would probably not get sick if they would heed their bodies' calls to get rest, exercise, or proper food and water.

The second step in self-discovery is through the senses. Often we do not pay enough attention to the information that comes to us through our senses. There are so many stimuli, especially of sight and sound, that we tend to block out everything! But such blocking narrows our perception of the world. After all, the only way we can truly know our world is through our senses. Even for urban dwellers, there is a wealth of colors, sounds, smells, tastes, and feels that can enrich our lives. My spirit has often been uplifted on a city street to see a golden leaf spiraling slowly to earth from a twisted tree. And the song of a mockingbird can penetrate to my ears even above the din of traffic—if my ears are open.

Begin to train your senses to do what they did when you were a child—give you all kinds of information. Even more important, train your mind to be open again to sensory perception.

Find yourself a pleasant place where there are grass and trees, and perhaps people, so long as they are not intrusively near. Settle down quietly, on a chair, a bench, or the grass. Then open your senses, one by one. Begin by looking carefully at everything you can see. Don't allow your eyes to pass quickly over familiar sights. Look at the different forms of grass blades, the delicate leaves of weeds, the way flower petals are formed. Pay attention to colors.

Then open your ears. Notice the breeze rustling the tree leaves. Listen to the sounds of birds, and observe how many different sounds you hear. You may be surprised to find that several species of birds are in your range of hearing. There will be insect noises and the voices of persons. Dwell on each of these.

Unlike lower animals, we usually do not use our sense of smell very much. You may have to bring some smells with you in order to use this sense. Perfumes, lotions, spices, and herbs can provide you with a pleasant sensation. But, as you continue to use your nose, you will discover aromas around you. Take these in and make them part of the new information you are gaining. Taste goes along with smell. Again, you may have to provide this for yourself. With all the chemicals we use today, it is not always safe to chew on a blade of grass. But you can bring some tasty bits to nibble. Do so slowly, reveling in the sense of taste. Be sure not to eat so much that your sense of taste is sated!

Touch or feel is the final sense. Touch the grass, the bark of a tree, the soil, sand, and any other object that interests you. It is a delightful exercise to close your eyes and explore by touch an object such as a stone or a twig.

Repeat this whole exercise, preferably in the same place, several times. You will be excited to see how much more you are able to perceive than you were the first time you sat down in this place. Then consciously set yourself to see, hear, smell, taste, and touch what is around you on all occasions. You will feel more alive and more in tune with the world as you do this.

Now that you are growing to know yourself, you can find ways of enjoying yourself while alone. Do you have any hobbies or crafts that you can do alone? Self-stimulation is important to everyone. Simply sitting before the TV set is not the answer. You need activities that inform your mind, broaden your interests, or produce something creative. Reading books and magazines or watching informative TV programs can stimulate your mind and broaden your interests. A public library card is a big help for everyone who wants to know more. Nature walks, bird-watching, or visits to local museums and parks can broaden your view of the world.

There are many hobbies and crafts that can be done with much pleasure and little outlay of money: Macrame, leatherworking, woodworking, needlepoint, other needlework, latch-hook rug making, gemstone polishing are only a few of the hobbies available.

Perhaps your alone times, although lonely, may be of brief duration. This certainly will be true if you have a family or a demanding job. So choose hobbies which you can pick up and lay down quickly. It is better to do leatherworking than cabinet making if you only have an hour or two to spend. Otherwise, you may take so much time getting ready to work that you have little time left for the creative part of your hobby.

While you are enjoying yourself, you are also making yourself more interesting to others. The broader one's interests, the more people one can relate to. And other persons enjoy knowing someone who has wide interests.

As you do all these things for yourself, continue to affirm your own self-worth. Congratulate yourself on the ways you are enhancing your life. Display your work to your family and friends. Enter a hobbies fair if one is available. Talk to yourself about what you are learning. Some of these suggestions may seem to be childish, but they are not. They are the ways that help persons grow in self-esteem. Remember that you should get 25 percent of your meaningful personal contacts from yourself!

Be Creative in Solitude

Every person has creative gifts. This is part of being made in the image of God. He is the great Creator. So anyone made in his image must also be creative. But many people, because they do not have certain talents which they perceive as creative, do not think of themselves as gifted. In conferences, I have often asked persons to list talents and then to state which talents they had. In most cases, the participants would list talents which they could not imagine themselves having!

Whatever expresses a person's own individuality is creative. Visit a crafts fair. Notice how many people have taken a basic craft and added their own touches. These crafts then become individual, so that anyone seeing the product would know immediately who had crafted it if the artisan was known to the observer.

Creative ideas are as numerous as there are creative people. Here are just a few ways to use creative gifts: growing plants (greenhouses and gardens), cooking, sewing, building machines and models, inventing things, drawing, painting, singing, playing a musical instrument, decorating, landscape gardening, cabinetmaking, woodcarving, all kinds of handicrafts, and photography.

When you visit a crafts fair, look at the basic form and then imagine how you would alter it. What materials would you add? How would its shape or use differ?

Actually, imagination is the main ingredient of creativity. This is a faculty we have from our childhood. Often it is shoved aside or buried under our concern for logic and "education" as we grow older. But it is never totally lost. It can be recovered and put to use throughout life. Persons like Grandma Moses who expressed creativity in new ways late in life testify to that fact.

I well remember the childhood fantasy that set my feet on the long road to being a writer. I was in the third grade and walking to school. A small pile of sand and gravel caught my eye. It had been eroded by the rains so that some of the sparkling mica and rose-colored pebbles extended above the rest of the pile. To my enchanted eyes these pebbles looked like the tiny palaces of a fairy city. Later at school I wrote an essay on my "fairy place." The teacher praised it highly. Through her encouragement I began to write some more. Other teachers and friends helped me over the years. Like most people, it was difficult to conceive of myself as a writer. I could say, "I write"; but I would not say, "I am a writer."

After my first husband died, I began to travel. I realized that I seemed to notice things other people didn't. I was the one who caught sight of two lambs beside a black mountain pool high above the snow line in Norway. I was the one who ventured to sample some of the unknown tastes of Scandinavian and Scottish cooking. I noticed turtledoves in Israel and wondered what kind of bird had black wings and a powder-blue tail. The Arab children in Nazareth looked to me as the child Jesus might have looked. And I savored the water from Mary's Well in that village. Perhaps, I thought, it tasted the way it did when Mary drew it for her household.

At last I was able to face and admit the truth: Yes, I am a writer, a creative person dealing with words. Imagination plus the ability to use all my senses marked me as that. For this is what is needed to be creative: imagination plus the ability to observe the world in a fresh way.

You can use a modification of the sensory exercise described earlier to sharpen your imagination. Transport yourself to a different world in imagination. Choose a favorite place which you loved as a child. Or picture yourself in some exotic place which you have visited or would like to visit. Make yourself comfortable—on the beach, under a flowering lilac tree, in a hammock—anywhere outside. Then conjure up in your imagination the most vivid or restful colors, the most exciting or delicate sounds, the most interesting smells and tastes, the feel and touch of objects that set your fingers tingling. Do this exercise when you want to arouse creativity or when you just want to have a "happy trip." "Getting high" on drugs is not to be compared to what your own imagination can do when you give it freedom. And there are certainly no terrible aftereffects!

If you want to be creative, make a place for that in your home. If it is only a corner, a desk, or a small workroom, fix it up. Hang pictures that please your eye. Provide a radio or record player so that you can have music to create by. Bring fresh flowers or spray perfume if that pleases you. The more you are surrounded by creativity, the greater will be your incentive to create.

And remember that you are doing this for yourself. You need never share your creative results with anyone outside your family and close friends. But often creativity does grow into something that can be marketed. Many a person has built a second career out of a creative hobby.

Know God Better in Solitude

In chapter 3 much was said about the resources which God gives to his children. These are realized in the fellowship of the church, but they are most deeply appropriated in the silence with God. In the truest sense the resources of God are God himself. When he is present in our lives, we have available everything we need for triumphant daily living.

We might compare this to a child's dependence on a father. The father might send the child clothes, dispatch groceries to the house, and pay the rent and the utilities—all at a distance. But if the father is present, all these material resources will be supplied by him. Even more, the child will have the comforting, loving presence of the father.

The greatest joy of solitude with God is that he takes away our deepest loneliness. Human beings experience a certain kind of loneliness, even with their nearest and dearest. There are some experiences and thoughts that we cannot share even with our loved ones. These experiences may be too exalted or too debased for us to speak them out loud. If we should do so, we fear (perhaps rightly) that we would be misunderstood or even shunned. These feelings comprise what is called basic loneliness.

The true joy comes when we can open our hearts to our Heavenly Father through Jesus Christ. Our Father knows us, down to the last corpuscle and brain wave. There is nothing we can tell him that would shock him. There is tremendous relief in unburdening ourselves totally to one who both understands and loves.

At the same time that we offer him our deepest selves, he reveals himself to us on ever-deepening levels. Though infinitely far above us, he is also intimately close to us. He makes himself known to us in our silences.

This communion, when it comes, is the most satisfying we can know. Augustine wrote, "Thou hast made us for Thyself, and our hearts are restless till they find their rest in Thee." We are God's children, created to have fellowship with him, just as Adam and Eve did in the Garden. Often we do not know this truth, or we have forgotten it. So we spin around in circles, hunting for human companionship or human love to fill the ache in our spirits. But we never find rest until we have come to find it in God.

How can we use our alone times to have this kind of communion with God? Those who have come closest all agree on certain basic preconditions: We must shut out the world and concentrate our minds on him. We must be willing to do his will and be open to his direction for our lives. We must not set conditions on the way he will reveal himself or on the way we will see him. We must let him be himself to us. This may mean that we may not have the kind of revelation we are looking for. But if we are truly seeking his will, the revelation will come. This condition is unchangeable: first the obedience, then the revelation.

You can shut out the world and concentrate on God through using one of the relaxation exercises suggested earlier in this chapter. It is important to drain out the tension which has been built up in daily living. When this is done, you can more easily clear your mind of earthly thoughts and worries.

Those who have practiced this kind of clearing exercise suggest that the worshiper imagine herself in a beautiful and beloved place. This is the same kind of suggestion given in the "creative fantasy" exercise. When you are there, imagine that Jesus comes to be with you. Allow him to be present with you just as a friend. This is not the time for petitions but for opening to communion.

To concentrate on God, fix your mind on a favorite verse of Scripture, or imagine Jesus speaking some of his words to you. As you empty your mind, you will find new insights coming to you from the Scriptures, or from the depths of your spirit.

You will be aware of areas in your life where you need to obey God more completely. This is the time for confession and surrender to God's will. Jesus said that we prove our love to God through obedience (John 14:15). Since this is a communion of love, it is important to be sure that you are expressing your love to God through your obedience. Nor does God's will have to be some great thing, some extraordinary sacrifice. What he wants from us is our willingness to follow his guidance moment by moment. That is harder than making one great sacrifice! But it is the path of love and power.

Perhaps there will be no great revelation in the time of

quietness. That is not necessary. God must be God and reveal himself in his own way and time. Our part is to clear the path of communion and obedience. We are promised his power as we do his will. So the revelation may come unexpectedly—but always when we need it the most.

The revelation also comes, I believe, in line with our own personalities. Just yesterday I was practicing this time of communion in silence. I had pictured myself sitting on a veranda of a cottage above the Adriatic Sea. Bright boungainvillea blossoms trailed across the horizontal framework above my head. Heavy clusters of dark blue grapes hung down, close enough for my hand to reach them. As I popped the grapes into my mouth, Jesus quietly came to sit beside me.

I was concentrating on the verse I had found the night before: "Where the Spirit of the Lord is, there is freedom" (2 Cor. 3:7, RSV). Jesus began to speak to me of freedom as a butterfly, floating freely through the air. The breeze that bore the butterfly, he told me, was the Spirit. The butterfly was surrounded by the air, borne by it, and directed by it. This was what freedom could mean to me. I think the image of the butterfly came to me because it is my favorite symbol. I wear butterfly jewelry almost invariably. Through some familiar imagery, then, I received new and valuable insights on the way to be free through the power and guidance of the Spirit of God.

When we find God, we also find all the resources of God in new and vital forms. We find peace as power in reserve. Who would not be able to have peace so long as he or she knew that there was power in reserve to meet every threat and every emergency? We find trust as the antidote for fear. We trust the Lord in communion with him, not only to reveal himself to us but also to make every day a triumph. We learn patience as we "wait upon the Lord." And we find new self-control as we empty our lives before him.

We learn to know what it feels like to be both loved by God and rendered lovable by him. Notice how women and men bloom when they are in love. To find that someone loves them is the best tonic and beauty treatment combined. So, as we experience the love of God, we become more lovable—to all those around us.

Most of all, we experience joy. A confession of faith says: "The chief end of man is to glorify God and enjoy him forever." It seems strange to put those two verbs together. How does glorifying God lead to enjoying him? It would seem that God would enjoy us in our glorification of him. But God is the author of joy. Knowing him, being like him, glorifying him will bring us the depths and heights of joy that we can know in no other way. As the psalmist said, "In thy presence there is fullness of joy, in thy right hand are pleasures for evermore" (16:11, RSV).

Learn from Your Lonely Times

Times of being alone and lonely can be important teachers. As you discover yourself, you may find unpleasant parts that need to be eliminated if you are going to find friends. In your confession times with God, you will find spots of anger, fear, resentment, and coldness. These will keep you from relationships.

When you find these aspects in your personality, don't allow yourself to give up in disgust. Instead, commit these areas to God. Make it part of your moment-by-moment obedience to be aware of the times when you feel angry, fearful, cold, depressed, resentful, and distant. Learn step by step to eliminate these from your life.

Also, notice whether you have a great number of alone times. If they seem out of proportion, work to fill these times with relationships. These needn't be deep friendships. Perhaps just someone you can talk with on coffee break or a call during the lull in a morning routine will give your spirit the lift it needs.

In your alone times, you will often feel the pain of loneliness. But as you practice making yourself your best friend and learning to know God, who truly is your best friend, this pain will give place to glory. Then you will know that alone times can be some of the most meaningful periods of your life.

Note

1. Austin Kutscher, ed., *But Not to Lose* (New York: Fredrick Fell, Inc., 1969), p. 28.

8

Grow into a Caring Person

The path out of loneliness is not complete without taking one more step. The lonely person may learn to feel that he or she is worthy of love. He or she can learn to make and keep friends and find a place in a caring community. But without the last step such a person is still essentially lonely. For the bottom line of loneliness is that persons keep saying, "I want someone to care about me." That attitude is one of self-concern. Whenever such a person encounters a change in circumstances, the loss of some cherished friends, or an internal lack of confidence, the loneliness will surface. Again the cry will be, "Why doesn't someone care about me?"

That line needs to be changed to: "I want to care about someone." This attitude is the outgoing, loving stance that reachs out to others. It does not wait for others to reach out. It is willing to take risks for the sake of relationships. The person with this attitude may experience periods of loneliness, as everyone does. But he or she will not be a lonely person.

Many people move to this step naturally. As they experience the love and fellowship of others, they become free to care. But for others this step may take an act of will and the deliberate cultivation of caring. Certain elements are needed in order to become a caring person. Some of these have already been stated in other chapters. But it will be helpful to review them.

Be secure in your sense of self-worth. The more you feel worthy of love, the freer you will feel to give love to others.

Be sure you are getting a healthy balance of meaningful personal contacts: from yourself, 25 percent; from your close family and friends, 20 percent; and from all others, 55 percent. It is only as you keep your bank account full of these warm contacts that you can risk spreading love all around. There is no scarcity of love. But to believe that and act on it requires a full intake of love.

Continue to tune out the old alarm systems and other unhealthy conditioning from your childhood. This will take a lifetime. But one sign that you are becoming more mature as a person is that you are increasingly ready to act on what you know now, not on what you picked up as a child.

Find a secure place in a loving community, and deepen those relationships. Everyone needs a home base. In our first home base, we learned about relationships with persons. As we have seen, some of the things we learned were healthy, and some were harmful. In our new home base, the caring community, we learn new ways of relating. Some of them will undergird our earlier teaching. Some of them will be contrary to our childhood conditioning. Whatever we learn and practice of healthy relationships in that community can be carried over into our relationships with other persons. These may be lonely persons within the community or ones outside the community whom we care about.

In addition to the community, have a good number of friends on all levels, as suggested in chapter 6. A person who puts all his or her friendship eggs in one basket is too busy juggling that basket to reach out to others.

Once I knew a woman with that problem. She made few friends, and she put a heavy load of dependence on them. Whenever one of her friends moved away or died, she was desolate. She refused to heed the advice that she broaden the scope of her friendships. Instead, she transferred all her eggs from one "basket'' to the next. Through the years, instead of becoming more involved and having more friends, her circle diminished. At last even the friends she had became less interested in her. She would not make efforts to contact them, leaving the initiative to them. And they dropped their efforts. Finally she was left with only her family, and they took little notice of her. By concentrating on her one basket, she had lost friendships rather than increasing them. There was no way for her to become a caring person.

In addition to self-esteem, cultivate a healthy self-love. Read again the definition of self-love in chapter 3. Observe where you need to grow in this kind of love for yourself and for others. The more you devote yourself to the "ends of God" in your personality, the better able you will be to see "the ends of God" in another person. When we see persons in this way, we are better able to care for them and about them.

As you increase your self-love, you will have inner energy to use all the parts of your personality. (Review these in chapter 5.) Love is energy. God's love flows into us, empowering us with his energy. This power can flow through you, making it possible for you to devote all your personal qualities to healthy living. Think of the ways your personality "star" can be used in caring for others.

You can think about others, getting information about them and from them. You can care about others, not only to give them protection if they need it but also to provide them with permission to be themselves. You can expand your values to include the qualities of caring and to recognize the importance of caring. You can give yourself to the emotions of caring, which are trust, hope, and love. And you can reduce your dependence on your old learned responses as you risk caring.

As you reach out to others, watch your attitude. It needs to remain in an "I'm OK—you're OK" spot. One problem with caring about others is that it can degenerate into "taking care of" others. This kind of attitude does not show respect for persons. It does not take into account their competence to care for themselves. It makes them victims.

Caring means: I respect you as a person. I salute your difference from me. I am willing to let you be different, even to the point of making mistakes, even as I make mistakes. I love you for who you are, and I am willing to devote energy to helping you to become the best person you can be, with your special personal qualities. This is the healthy caring attitude.

Review the four elements which friends can supply (see the beginning of chapter 6). How well do you stack up on being that friend, as well as looking for that kind of friend? Are you willing to share the concerns of others? Or do you see only your own concerns? Are you dependable in a pinch? Can a friend call you on short notice to take care of an emergency? Are you able to be a friend in whom a person can confide, knowing that this information will be kept? Can the friend be sure that you will neither betray the confidence nor hold it against him? Do you respect the competence of others to handle their own lives? These questions are all different ways of stating the caring attitude. As you answer them, you may see gaps where you can become more mature as a friend.

Remember that the essentials of close friendship are understanding and dialogue (see chapter 6). Assess yourself as to how willing you are to expend energy in these ways of sharing. If you find yourself drawing back, don't hit yourself over the head. Instead, retrace the steps of gaining energy through warm contacts and a loving community. There is nothing more draining than trying to give understanding and engage in dialogue when you really don't feel like it. Energy for sharing comes from the love that is generated within you through the love of God and others.

Most of all, learn more from Jesus about the love that

cares. Two of the greatest statements about Jesus' caring love, to me at least, are found in the Gospel of John.

At the beginning of John 13, we read the account of Jesus' washing the disciples' feet. This was not a religious ritual; it was a daily necessity. Persons in Palestine did not sit down to eat with unwashed feet. The roads were dusty, and the people wore sandals. Washing the feet was a servant's task. But there was no servant present in the upper room. The disciples, concerned about their image, would not stoop to handle this menial task.

But look at Jesus: "Well aware that the Father had entrusted everything to him, and that he had come from God and was going back to God" (v. 3),[1] he was willing to act as a servant. His sense of self-worth, rooted in his relationship to the Father, was not damaged by taking a servant's role. His self-love, devoted to the "ends of God" in his life, saw this task as another way of demonstrating his love to his disciples. He could engage in caring love because he did not have to worry about his image.

The second episode in John's Gospel involves Jesus' teaching about friendship (John 15:12-15). Jesus commanded his disciples to love one another with Jesus' kind of love. This is a deeper love even than the love of neighbor. This is self-sacrificing love, caring even to the point of death if necessary. Jesus was at the point of demonstrating this love for his disciples. So he now called them friends.

Further, he described this love as one of dialogue or sharing: "I call you servants no longer; a servant does not know what his master is about. I have called you friends, because I have disclosed to you everything that I heard from my Father" (v. 15, NEB).

Jesus urged the disciples to demonstrate their love for him by keeping his commandments. We might interpret this as asking for a love of action rather than words. It is easy to say that we care for others. It is much harder to act that way. But Jesus did. He showed love in every action of his life, and he called on his disciples to do the same.

Anyone who wants to grow into a caring person might do well to make the prayer of Francis of Assisi a daily challenge:

> Lord, make me an instrument of your peace.
>> Where there is hatred, let me sow love.
>> Where there is injury, pardon,
>> Where there is doubt, faith,
>> Where there is despair, hope,
>> Where there is darkness, light, and
>> Where there is sadness, joy.
> O Divine Master, grant that I may not so much
>> seek to be consoled, as to console;
>> To be understood, as to understand;
>> To be loved, as to love;
>> For it is in giving that we receive—
>> It is in pardoning that we are pardoned;
>> It is in dying that we are born to
>> eternal life.

Note

1. From *The New English Bible.* Copyright © The Delegates of the Oxford University Press and the Syndics of the Cambridge University Press, 1961, 1970. Reprinted by permission. Subsequent quotations are marked NEB.